The Human Side of Teaching

The Human Side of Teaching

Being the Caring Teacher You Want to Be

Francis J. Gardella

ROWMAN & LITTLEFIELD
Lanham • Boulder • New York • London

Executive Acquisitions Editor: Tom Koerner
Assistant Acquisitions Editor: Jasmine Holman
Sales and Marketing Inquiries: textbooks@rowman.com
Published by Rowman & Littlefield
An imprint of The Rowman & Littlefield Publishing Group, Inc.
4501 Forbes Boulevard, Suite 200, Lanham, Maryland 20706
www.rowman.com

86-90 Paul Street, London EC2A 4NE

British Library Cataloguing in Publication Information Available

Library of Congress Cataloging-in-Publication Data

Names: Gardella, Francis J., author.
Title: The human side of teaching : being the caring teacher you want to be / Francis J. Gardella.
Description: Lanham, Maryland : Rowman & Littlefield Publishers, 2023. | Includes bibliographical references. | Summary: "The book addresses several areas of the classroom/school community with which educators must deal as they pursue their dream of being a good teacher and colleague"—Provided by publisher.
Identifiers: LCCN 2023030757 (print) | LCCN 2023030758 (ebook) | ISBN 9781475873313 (cloth) | ISBN 9781475873320 (paperback) | ISBN 9781475873337 (epub)
Subjects: LCSH: Classroom environment. | Teacher–student relationships. | Parent–teacher relationships. | Teachers—Professional relationships.
Classification: LCC LB3013 .G344 2023 (print) | LCC LB3013 (ebook) | DDC 371.102/3—dc23/eng/20230727
LC record available at https://lccn.loc.gov/2023030757
LC ebook record available at https://lccn.loc.gov/2023030758

♾️™ The paper used in this publication meets the minimum requirements of American National Standard for Information Sciences—Permanence of Paper for Printed Library Materials, ANSI/NISO Z39.48-1992.

As with all things I do or attempt, I must dedicate this book to my wife, Gail. Through the many years of our life together, she has been the constant inspiration for all my work. Her continued support always has me looking ahead for the next opportunity, challenge, or whatever is to be. Her constancy in all this is what places me where I am today.

A book on the human side of education must also be dedicated to Jim Williams. Now if you knew JR, you would know that the title of the book fits right into the way he saw education: as a human experience. His ideas of what truly creates a school community can never be forgotten and, while trying, can never be duplicated. His uniqueness as an educator had an incredibly positive impact on so many and moved them to see the profession as a human endeavor.

Contents

Preface

Writing what my book is about gives me an opportunity to put forth my reasons for writing and some important aspects of the book. However, when an author finds someone who states these points so much better, the ego must be set aside and bring forth this giant. This is just the position in which I find myself. For me, one of these giants is Robert Fulghum. I first "met" Mr. Fulghum when a colleague, Phil Caccavale, brought me a list of ideas from Fulghum's well known book *All I Really Needed to Know I Learned in Kindergarten*. This led me to read more of Fulghum including *Uh-Oh*. (Yes, that is the name of his book.) In this book, Fulghum relates something that I feel sets a tone for what I am presenting.

He discusses his visits to kindergartens and colleges. He relates that environments differ only in scale. In both places, you find materials for learning, reading, science, and the arts. However, the difference he finds is the placement. With younger children, all these materials are in the same classroom. In colleges, as we know, the resources are scattered all over the campus.

But in Fulghum's judgment, the difference is in the self-image of the students. He found that kindergarten students feel that they can do anything: Sing, dance, draw, be poetic, and learn to count.

"Their answer is Yes! Over and over again, Yes! The children are confident in spirit, infinite in resources, and eager to learn. Everything is still possible."

But when it comes to college students, he found people who "know their limitations." "I only play piano, I only draw horses, I only dance to rock and roll, I only sing in the shower." He found that one of the major reasons for this was that these college students seem to be "embarrassed for others to see them sing or dance or act."

Fulghum sums this writing up with a query that should make us all think about what we do. He writes, "What went wrong between kindergarten and college? What happened to 'YES! Of course I can!'?" (Fulghum 1991, 225–227)

Well dear readers, one of the major impacts on children between kindergarten and college is a group of people known as teachers. This group of people, whether neophytes or veterans, affects every person who moves through the grades. So, what I try to do here is have us think about and reconsider the goals, objectives, and attitudes for ourselves, our students, and those who create a school community. It is my hope that what you read will help you to discover this.

Introduction

An experienced educator sits across a table at the local coffee shop, speaking with a teacher who is working through a difficult time in their career, whether in the first few months or after a good number of years in the classroom. This person states that the goal of becoming a teacher was to help children. They did not sign on to spend a great deal of time completing detailed lesson plans in a certain format; conducting their lessons in a structured (nay, I say, a preassigned) model; and giving up the individualism that they saw as their major contribution to education. And yet today, many teachers are doing just those things, especially those still trying to come out of two years of remote instruction (we know we cannot call it remote learning) with their children.

My purpose here is to portray many ideas for the people issues with which doubting teachers have to deal (and overcome) to become the educators they want to be. For experienced teachers, *The Human Side of Teaching* can rekindle the teacher they once were and link them to that time when their career was new. These people are encountering the profession in an age of scripted curriculum, overly specific educational standards while addressing faces in boxes on a screen. It truly is not what they signed up for. They need to remember the zeal in entering teaching, the humanity they envisioned in teaching, and the human beings with whom they are dealing. And this is the focus of *The Human Side of Teaching*.

From a district perspective, education continues to focus on national and state standards, but teachers need to hear that their chosen profession gives them the opportunity to have an impact on the lives of their students and not just be a content speaker and test preparer. They need to know that teaching remains a human endeavor, although it may not seem like it on many days. Teachers need to focus on the people with whom they deal (themselves, their students, their supervisors, and many others in the school community) to be successful as teachers.

While the setting may be a conversation with a teacher, the focus of this writing is to show the importance of established teachers understanding that teaching is about them and their success in helping children—in a sense, the way it used to be (or at least the way they thought it was supposed to be). *The Human Side of Teaching* offers the observations of a classroom teacher, district supervisor, and now college faculty member with a great number of years of experience dealing with teachers (even himself) in urban, rural, and suburban settings. Its premise is that good teaching begins with the teacher's thoughts about themselves and those with whom they work. This also serves as a reminder that good teaching is not about those ideas from multiple influencers, about the "experts'" directions, or the way it should be done.

The aim of this book is to have teachers address issues so that the passion they had to be great teachers is developed (or rekindled) and so they have a positive impact on their students, avoiding robotic teaching based on "expert" opinions and the one-size-fits-all curriculum and assessments. For some, this may be another opportunity to hear about *The Human Side of Teaching.*

1

About You

1.1. LET YOUR TEACHING ALLOW YOU TO
EXPRESS YOUR PASSION FOR WHAT YOU DO

Begin each lesson as if it is *the most important lesson* you will ever teach. Let your passion for your chosen profession shine through. With this, good days will be fantastic, and bad days will go better than expected. You are the person who sets your expectations.

Begin each lesson with enthusiasm, as if it is *the first lesson* you have ever conducted. As you begin the session, remember the passion (as well as some of the nervousness) you had in your first lesson, whether as a teacher, student teacher, or intern. Remember this as the good side of tension that keeps us improving.

Begin each lesson as if it is *the last lesson* you will ever teach. (No gallows humor here, like "Thank goodness, I can now retire." That's not the teacher you want to be.) Focus on what you want to impress on your students about the content, but also and maybe more importantly, emphasize why learning is so important for your students, both now and later. Your passion for teaching will show your students that your goal is to help them.

1.2. YOUR STUDENTS WILL FEEL YOUR
SPIRIT IF YOU DO NOT TRY TO HIDE IT

During each lesson, the spirit within you is a constant barometer of your work. If your spirit is weak, then so are you, and so goes your lesson. If your spirit is strong, then it will drive you to be better at what you do. Let this spirit and your energy for teaching come through. Let the students understand that you want them to learn and that, for you, teaching is a very important thing to do.

Try not to tell this to your students. Many times, students have heard this before and have been disappointed by the results. Over the course of the year, portray your zest for teaching so that no student can ignore or disregard it. They may not react how you wish, but you cannot allow their reactions to mold your passion and attitude. Remember that whether they accept this or not is up to them, but bring it to them and give them that choice. Don't allow outside negativity stop you from giving this to your students.

1.3. LOVE YOUR SUBJECT, BUT LOVE YOUR STUDENTS MORE!

Your passion for ideas and subjects brought you to teaching so others can learn what you love, and your continued learning keeps you alert to new ideas. Show these to your students. More so, show them that they are loved and that you want them to succeed in learning so they can succeed in life. Your teaching is more about your students than the content.

Yes, you want them to learn concepts and facts, but you also want them to know that they are still considered good people even if they have problems with the learning. This is especially true for students who have difficulty learning and, in their frustration, act negatively toward you and the class. The art of teaching is about having students love to learn, and that love is developed through the subjects you teach. In this, they must know that they are accepted by you even if they are not scholars. They are accepted by you because they want to learn, regardless of whether they are good at it.

1.4. ON BEING TIRED

We all get tired, but remember, there is good tired and bad tired. Such an idea is heard in the words of singer/songwriter Harry Chapin's grandfather, an artist who illustrated Robert Frost's first two books of poetry. Chapin related in an interview that his grandfather told him,

> Ironically enough, bad tired can be a day that you won. But you won other people's battles, you lived other people's days, other people's agendas, other people's dreams. And when it was all over there was very little you in there. And when you hit the hay at night, somehow you toss and turn—you don't settle easy.

. . . Good tired, ironically enough, can be a day that you lost. But you don't even have to tell yourself because you knew you fought your battles, you chased your dreams, you lived your days. And when you hit the hay at night, you settle easy, you sleep the sleep of the just and you can say, take me away. . . . Harry, all my life I've wanted to be a painter. And I've painted. God, I would have loved to have been more successful. But I've painted, and I've painted, and I am good tired, and they can take me away. (Chapin 1988)

There are going to be days when your tired is good, which you should accept, and days when it is bad, which you should try to avoid. Make sure you are always on the lookout for those things that will make you good tired. They come in many forms, and sometimes they are not the easiest way to go. Be consciously aware of avoiding (if possible) things that will make you bad tired. Events that lead you to be good tired will make you feel accomplished and successful because they are you, even if you lose.

1.5. NEVER DEFEAT YOURSELF

On any Sunday, any professional football team can defeat any other team. The defeated team does not think they will then be defeated in the next game. They just lost one game, and that does not tell them about the future. (Obviously some fans do not feel this way, but they are not the professionals.) Professionals take a setback, learn from it, and move toward success in the very next endeavor.

When a class does not go well, and possibly when a whole day does not go well, do not project that defeat onto the next. Take a breath, gather your passion and your spirit, and have them ready for success tomorrow. Reignite your energy in planning. This may call for you going to others you trust and asking for assistance. You only become a poor teacher when you allow circumstances to control your destiny. You need to control your destiny, no matter the circumstances.

Having the attitude of "failing is not going to happen again" is what makes people successful. Will failing happen again? Of course it will. But each time you must be aware that, as difficult as it may be, you cannot accept it as continuing.

1.6. CONTINUE TO BE INTELLECTUAL, NO MATTER WHAT YOU TEACH

You teach subjects you have known for a long time, whether you teach several as an elementary teacher or a single subject to older children. For you, the actual content that you teach should not be a challenge. (By the way, if it is, then you have homework to do.)

However, learning the content may be a challenge for your students, so approach it as something worthwhile to be learned. To truly understand the vantage point of your students, continually challenge yourself to learn more about your field. Don't become more conversant with the content you teach, but challenge yourself to learn more, even if it has little or no impact on your actual teaching.

The depth at which one can study a subject is almost limitless. For example, in history, what is the impact of individual people on events or the impact of events on individual people? In language arts, what in a poet's makeup possibly led to an astonishing work? What about that mathematician who developed an idea? Was that scientific discovery a result of research or an unexpected event? (See the history of penicillin.)

Choose a part of your content area, and search for new knowledge. It is a deep knowledge of a content area that allows one to be a creative teacher. As you know more of the foundational and deeper aspects of the content, you can begin to see many paths to what forms the school curriculum.

1.7. NEVER QUIT. WALK AWAY IF NECESSARY, BUT NEVER QUIT

Not all your teaching situations will be nirvanic. Some will be challenging, while others may be overwhelming. Be willing to assess your situation objectively. If you have a situation in which you find it difficult to cope, then prepare yourself to leave. Don't quit teaching; just move on to another environment. It is better to seek happiness than drag yourself through a situation in which you find it difficult to cope. Remember that it may not be you but the difficult situation in which others have put you, and you may not be willing or able to change it.

A principal I worked for once said to all the teachers new to the school, "You are here because we see you as good teachers. However, some of you may not fit well into the culture of our school, so you may not be here next year. But when you go to another school, you may find yourself being the excellent teacher you want to be." The key idea is that no one can truly say that you cannot do something. They can judge that you are not successful in a certain venue, but that is only one. There are always others. Remember, although you may want to blame yourself for everything (especially true for new teachers), your present school and culture just might not be a good match. So complete your job but then move on.

1.8. BEWARE THE IDES OF NOVEMBER

September of your first year of teaching is a time of feeling elation that you are a teacher and nervousness about doing a good job teaching and learning all the systems, formats, and organization of the school. But you are there. For you, the veteran teacher, it can be a new beginning: looking back on the last year and determining to make it better.

In October, your second month, you will find somewhat more of the same. You will begin to assess very directly how your teaching is affecting your students. However, at the same time, you may begin to have doubts about your career because your dream classroom may be meeting reality.

November truly brings a sense of "Have I made a mistake in thinking that I could teach?" Do not fight this. It is a natural consequence of the reality of teaching meeting your idealized view of teaching when you entered your school. Almost every new teacher goes through this. The idea of five days a week of doing what you are doing for at least seven more months may not be comforting to say the least.

Keep in mind that this will pass. December, January, and February will come and go. Suddenly you will find yourself in the spring of the year, and then, here comes the summer to rejuvenate and get ready for the next year. As the years go on, November will just become another month of school. But in order to have the summer to rejuvenate your teaching, you still have to be teaching, so do not let the ides of November get to you. Realizing they are coming is most important. Then it is a matter of facing up to them and moving on.

In fact, I once had a former student who sat in my office in November of her first year of teaching and cried about what was happening. With support from her colleagues, she made it through the year. In a visit to me the following November, I mentioned how different it was. When she asked, "Why?" I did not have the heart to remind her of the feelings she had about teaching just one year before. She seemed to have forgotten about dealing with the ides of November.

1.9. BE A PROFESSIONAL—WHATEVER THAT MEANS

Merriam-Webster defines *professional* as "exhibiting a courteous, conscientious, and generally businesslike manner in the workplace." From this definition, take the word *conscientious* to heart. This is the crux of your persona as a teacher. You will be courteous as a matter of course. Businesslike in teaching depends on circumstance. In the classroom, this may be warranted at times, although like any human endeavor, there are times when businesslike just does not fit what is happening, especially when dealing with children.

But conscientious is always there. Whether it is teaching a lesson or meeting with parents, students, peers, or supervisors, continue to be principled, honorable, and focused. Whether this is acceptable to others is not the issue. This is the only way true teachers can accept themselves.

1.10. BE YOURSELF, ALTHOUGH AT TIMES YOU MAY HAVE TO ACT

We all have models, those people or ideas we would love to follow. Remember, though, that the persona someone brings to a situation like teaching depends on one's personality and background. As there is a very good chance these will be different from yours, you must be careful about how strongly you follow any model.

The best way is to be yourself within the overall framework of a model. From the outset of your teaching, approach your classroom lessons with what is comfortable for you, as long as it proves to be effective. However, there are times when your personality or way of accomplishing your work may not be exactly what you need to do. In this case, *act*. Yes, that's correct, *act*. A good stage performer can take on many roles so the audience thinks that what they see is the performer's personality. However, many times that is not the case. Many performers are not like the characters they play. Many performers feel comfortable whether they are in an action movie or a Shakespearean play, and they seem to be different people in each case.

You also may need to become an actor. One role you need to play from day one is that of someone who knows what they are doing. This is vital because, in your school, the students may feel that they have more seniority than you have. Actually, this is true because a good many, if not all of them, have been there longer than you have. It is important that your role playing sends the message that you are a knowledgeable teacher who knows what to do. In your mind, you may be saying, "If they only knew how little I know," but the outward persona is an adult in charge who knows how to orchestrate the work of a classroom.

1.11. HAVE INTELLIGENCE; ENERGY; AND, MOST OF ALL, INTEGRITY

Merriam-Webster defines *integrity* as "firm adherence to a code." When you begin to teach, it is your intelligence (content and pedagogical knowledge) that will maintain you. Needless to say, your energy will get you through each day, week, month, and finally a school year. However, it is your integrity that makes you a true teacher. You need to maintain this throughout your career. Integrity is one of those attributes that keeps you true to yourself.

There will be times when your integrity will be challenged. There will be times when letting events take control may seem easier, especially before you receive tenure. However, remember that you still have to live with yourself. A colleague was let go by a district, and his final statement to the Board of Education was, "I came here with a bag of books and my integrity. I leave with a bag of books and my integrity." What more could a true professional say?

1.12. EXPECT TO BE SUCCESSFUL

What you think will happen helps to form the basis for what will really happen. Going into a classroom ready for success is fundamental to keeping your eyes on the prize: the success of your students. Be prepared to have your expectations challenged each day in the classroom and in the school. However, remember that challenges in any profession are expected. Do not allow them to blunt your expectations.

When you have a huge pile of papers to read or correct, expect to be successful in completing the task. (By the way, when faced with that pile, remember that the toughest thing about starting something is *to start*. In this case, that may mean reading or correcting the *first* paper.) All go through this. Some go through it for many years but keep on succeeding.

Your success depends upon your attitude as much as your circumstances. Your success in your second year of teaching depends on bettering your expectation of success in your first year. It is an expectation you cannot lose.

1.13. BE YOURSELF, NOT THE SELF OTHERS WANT YOU TO BE

There are many pressures on you, as a teacher, to do it "this way," "that way," or "not at all." These pressures come from all levels of a school community, including supervisors, colleagues, students, and parents. And there is a tendency for others to try to mold the newer people into what they see as being the best. But as you already know and possibly have faced in the past, someone else's best mold is not your mold.

This does not mean stand your ground and let them know where you stand! To be successful in a school community, you must be more subtle than that. You must accept that the way others see a situation is the way they see it, but you must let them know in a professional way that their view may not necessarily be your view. Doing this does not have be cataclysmic. Maintain your professional calm but let them know. Not all situations can be resolved in such a way. If it comes to a more robust response, then let it come, but do not make this your go-to response. Reserve it for when there is no other choice.

1.14. ALTHOUGH DIFFICULT AT TIMES, BE POSITIVE

The days and weeks in the life of a teacher have their ups and downs, and of course, there will be those who tell you that the ups are few and far between. But remember, this is common humor for those who have been in something for a long time, whether it is a job or even a marriage. Your responsibility is to remain positive no matter how difficult it is. For example, after all input is given, the school leadership may make a decision with which you do not agree. Unless there is an ethical or moral concern, try to accommodate the decision into your work.

It makes no sense to create in yourself a negative attitude about what is happening. Such an attitude just makes it more difficult to deal with the issue. Also, negative attitudes tend to remain with you throughout the day or week. It is sometimes the unseen baggage that we carry around, so let it go. This does not mean capitulate, nor does it mean change your ideals. It just means that a positive attitude toward a situation that is negative in your mind is better than a negative attitude toward a negative situation. Yes, in this case, two negatives do not make a positive. They merely thrive on each other.

1.15. BE TRUSTWORTHY WITH YOUR STUDENTS

Students expect a teacher to be teacher-like: focused on the lessons and the content. They also expect you to be a person as well as a teacher. Now you may say, "I am what I am," but students need to see you in both ways. As a person, they need to see you as trustworthy. Portray to them that there are many things that will occur in their school experience with you. Certainly, learning the content from the class is a very high priority. But also make sure you continually show them that you are a person they can trust, that you always are looking out for their best interests, and that their success in your class, as well as in school, is important to you.

From this, you can begin to make inroads into helping these young people for whom you are responsible. This may certainly be seen in their work in your class, but beyond that, you want them to see you as a person they can strive to become, not as a teacher in a school, but as a member of society. Remember, there are some students who do not have positive adult role models in their lives. Try to show what mature adults should be like.

1.16. ACCEPT THAT SOMETIMES YOU WILL FAIL

There are many ideas about failing in education. First, while failure is not preferable, it is a possibility, and it is more of a possibility than most people wish to admit. As a person, you must be ready to face failure and plan your next steps. When it comes to time allocation, more time is needed to focus on planning the next steps. Pondering that you failed at something does not change it, nor does it set the stage for improvement.

Ask anyone who is involved in a competitive field. Take the plight of a hockey goalie who has just allowed a goal. She cannot continue to think about her mistake because *here they come again.* So also in a classroom. While your first thought if something goes wrong is to mull over what you did, you must avoid this because, when you look up, the students are still there. We know that failure is part of being a human, but this does not bring any relief at the time of the failure, so realize that it happened, that you will do your best to not have it happen again, and then move on.

And be careful of using failure as a positive force. Many times, teachers try to respond to students with something like, "Don't worry. If you are wrong, it could be a learning experience." However, and I know this from my own experience, when those same teachers are in their own classes at the college or in professional development or in a faculty meeting, failure is not an option in their peer group. So be careful of preaching something you do not practice.

1.17. SARCASM ONLY LEADS TO PLACES
YOU DO NOT WANT TO GO

The responses that you give to people, especially students, need to be what you would expect to receive back from them. Holding yourself to a high standard, you can use your acceptable responses when they answer inappropriately (and they will). Teachers tend to lose the high ground on this when they continually use sarcasm. Students, being immature, will follow your lead, and if your lead is a sarcastic attitude toward them, then the interaction will end up in verbiage with which you do not want to deal.

We all know that sarcasm is sometimes seen as humor. The people on many talk shows that students watch use sarcasm to denigrate the target of the hour. This is also true in how people use social media. Students know this, and they may even use it themselves among themselves. Be that as it may, your use of this type of speech can only degrade your position as an adult, a teacher, and a leader, roles you must play in a school, whether you wish to or not. So be careful, and when faced with such, do not return in kind. Change the direction to let students know that such speech is unacceptable, as it may be hurtful to some, even though others find it amusing.

2

About You Leading as a Classroom Teacher

2.1. YOU CAN LEAD EVEN IF YOU ARE NOT IN CHARGE

Even though you are not the appointed leader of a team, grade-level committee, and so on, you can still lead. Continue to be part of the discussion at all times, and offer suggestions you see as necessary. Do not expect your ideas or suggestions to be accepted all the time, but by remaining in the conversation, you will blend your ideas with those of others to hopefully make progress.

In these cases, be in conversation with others about the ideas, even when you are not at a formal meeting. Many times, these are the discussions that allow others to see your point and adjust their view. It also gives you an opportunity to review their viewpoint and possibly modify yours. In this, people will see you not only as someone with ideas but also as someone who wishes to move forward.

There is a somewhat dismal statement that a committee's only real decision is to how to keep the committee meeting. In a sense, this means keeping a committee in existence is the main focus of the committee at all times. So in your work to resolve an issue, a number of people may be inwardly thankful for your work in helping to find a solution, thereby getting them off the committee. And next time, they may look to see what you think before they make a decision.

2.2. CONTRIBUTE YOUR IDEAS, NO
MATTER HOW THEY ARE RECEIVED

In a discussion, there are times when the group is really headed in one direction, and you may find yourself thinking a little differently. When you voice your thoughts, they might not be met with the kind of acceptance that you thought they would be. There are many reasons for this, from going against group think to being seen as too young, different, or complicated. Such an experience should not deter you from continuing to put forth your ideas. Although the group did not agree with you, the notion that you have thought about the situation differently may set up more thought on your comments down the road. This is especially true for new teachers.

New teachers are considered neophytes who are there to learn. For some, the idea that new teachers may have a valid idea is fogged over by the fact that they are new or young. However, promoting your views may lead to a trail of thinking about what you say—maybe not this time but a little down the road. In a sense, you have planted the seed with others that you have ideas they may want to consider. Sometimes it is okay to go along, and sometimes, you may want to implant the idea that a different direction is possible. As author George Bernard Shaw says, "The reasonable adapts himself to the world; the unreasonable persists in trying to adapt the world to himself. Therefore, all progress depends on the unreasonable man" (Shaw 1902).

2.3. LEADING IS CREATING SPACE
FOR LEARNERS TO LEARN

Robert Altman, an Oscar-winning director, said that the "role of a director is to create a space where actors and actresses can become more than they have ever been before, more than they have ever dreamed of being" (Peters and Green 2022). As the leader in your classroom, this is your focus. In synchronizing the content with your students, you need the students to realize what they can learn. Many times, students will enter your classroom with a fixed mindset of what they are able to do and not do. This mindset is usually formed from what they have heard from others, especially older friends and siblings who have already been there. "Wait until you get Ms. Smith" or "Don't even think you are going to pass geometry" are some of the ideas banging around in the heads of some of your students when they enter your class.

What your classroom needs to become is a place where such ideas are seen as fantasies or tall tales rather than reality, where the students are shocked that they can learn to be successful with constructive persistence. Even if they think they are not necessarily bright or smart, they should be able to open themselves up in the learning space that you provide for them daily. This is not easy for a teacher to do, but it is a commitment to a goal toward which you want to lead your students.

2.4. LEADERS HAVE IMPACT THROUGH THE DECISIONS THEY MAKE

As a leader in the classroom, you make many decisions. While doing this, you need to consider a very important idea. You must consider how your supervisors will view your decisions and how they will affect your students. Sometimes, the impact of your decision on these two audiences will be very different. Where the leadership may think it fits into their view of what the school should look like, the students may see it as leaving them out in the cold. And if the students see your decisions as excellent, then the school leadership may call into question your membership in the school community.

For the most part, the far better thing to do is to consider your students first. If the leadership in the school calls your decisions into question, then explain in person to a principal or small number of administrators the reasons for your decisions. When the students question your decisions, it is much more difficult to explain it to them as a large group (four or five classes of maybe twenty-five students each). In the former, you have a chance to explain and answer questions from possibly each member of the group. In the latter, you basically lecture them about your decisions, with little if any time for discussion and with almost no time for everyone to be involved.

As a good leader, no matter the situation, you must give a great deal of consideration to those at a level lower than yours in the hierarchy. This is especially true when making decisions, for very often lower levels feel the impact far more than those above you in the hierarchy. It is caring that sometimes is forgotten.

2.5. LEADERS SERVE PEOPLE

As a classroom leader, you are not only responsible for what occurs, but you also must see yourself as serving, as best you can, what you wish to deliver to the people (students) in the class. Think about a time when you ordered food in an eatery, and although the food was served, the person in charge of the delivery seemed distant, as if your order was just one of a lot of others. For most people, this would be disconcerting. The missing human interaction is felt.

(An aside: For those who claim this is not true, wait a few years, when many services, such as waitstaff in an eatery or a purchase at a retail store, are done by robots. I wonder how many will begin to complain about the loss of the human touch. If you wish a more recent example, think of the number of places you are sent by an AI telephone system when you want to speak to a live person to order something or clear up a matter with a purchase.)

Your students are not truly clients because, for the most part, no matter the service, they cannot go to another school. Yet, this must not stop you from giving them the service that you would want to give if tomorrow they could go somewhere else to get what you are offering. Again, you serve "clients" while still being in charge of leading the class.

2.6. LEAD IN THE EXCITEMENT OF GETTING THINGS DONE

After all your years of schooling, getting something done can have the thrill of rain and a cloudy day. You've done it so often that only the major completions are noteworthy. Keep in mind that, because of your experience with content, this may be your view of classroom work. For your students, however, it is maybe the first time they are attempting something. As part of your classroom persona, make it all seem worthwhile. This is what students in many cases cannot or are not willing to do themselves, so they depend on you.

We know that many things we teach are not earth shattering. For us, they are the normal carrying on of the classroom, especially throughout the years of your career. For the sake of your students, keep this to yourself. While trying to make your classroom activities noteworthy, keep your energy level up so that, upon completion, the class thinks or believes that you see it (and therefore they possibly see it) as all worthwhile.

This is one of the most prominent roles you have as a teacher. Is it acting? Sometimes, especially when you have done the same thing in five different classes in one day, or you have done the same thing every year you have taught. However, if you feel your students need to understand something, then you need to get with it also and model an excitement of getting something done.

Even outside of the classroom, such activities as the performance of the class play or the publication of the yearbook are new experiences for the students, even if you have done these often as a teacher. Your excitement is necessary to show them the joy that should follow getting things done.

2.7. LEAD WITH YOUR VALUES

Look up the word *values*, and you will find it is something that a person feels is worthwhile and upholds. At the same time, you will be overrun with types, definitions, and lists of any number of values with accompanying images. More directly, a value is an idea that a person feels is paramount to their living in the world.

We know that values differ from person to person and therefore from teacher to teacher. However, this need not stop you from maintaining your values and using them to guide you in leading your students. It is not that you want your students to have your values. It is that you want your students to see that you have values, with the hope that they will see the strength in having values and developing their own.

Young people do not see the world as adults do. Many times, their actions are determined by adults, whether the young people like it or not. However, there will come a time when they no longer have that adult determination in their lives. It will be their time to stand for what they believe. For this reason, you as a leader must show them that you do have values, whether they agree with them or not, and the impact your values have on your life and how they set the stage for you to live in this world.

Case in point: Three young teachers were interviewed by a reporter for the school newspaper. They were asked, "What are your thoughts on abortion?" Their answers ranged from abortions on demand to when necessary to never. The student reporter, a young female, was surprised by the difference of views because all the men were younger teachers. The obvious lesson here is that, at any age, there are no group values, nor should there be. This is why you need to show your values in your persona.

2.8. HAVE YOUR CLASSROOM BECOME
A PLACE OF EMOTIONAL SAFETY

Being accepted is one of the basic tenets of emotional safety. The overriding force of competition may make some students feel that, because of their lack in some area of the topic, they are not accepted. It is the job of the teacher to have students see this differently. But keep in mind that children and adolescents sometimes are not very good at clearly seeing their place and acceptance level.

Without being too over the top, your work must focus on those who, from their experience, may think that they do not belong. Don't feel that you need to make them a star in the group; just make them feel that they are accepted as a person, and their words, whether agreeable or not, count. Many times, stating this to the group for all to hear still may not have an impact. It may just be a side conversation with a particular student, telling them that you know they are there.

While this is the way we would like to have it, there will be times when a student in your class does not have the background to feel comfortable in the group. Sometimes parental pressure may force a child into an academic situation for which they are not prepared. It is incumbent on you to do all you can to rectify the situation, but you must do so knowing that sometimes you cannot make things right. While you may feel that you as the teacher are the victim, you must realize that this will pass for you at the end of the school year, but the student will need to deal with this for a much longer time.

2.9. GOOD LEADERS ARE EMPATHETIC

Empathy is spoken about in many places. However, sometimes in a classroom, with the pressure of keeping twenty-five or more students moving forward, finishing the curriculum, and trying to ensure that test scores will be good, we can fall into the role of a bureaucrat (getting the job done) as opposed to a teacher (caring about more things in a classroom than we can name). At times, the pressure can make us quick in our language, too direct in our voice, and not understanding. While this will happen (and is sometimes beyond our control), you must make sure that you grasp the opportunity to be in contact with students as people when things are going well and make sure they are considered as more than just one of the group. Again, with the number of students each day (in your classes, the halls, etc.), this is difficult but important. And at times it does not take much. It may only take backing off on your authority and making sure that they are okay.

For example, I was walking down a school hallway during the change of classes, not exactly the time to be unaware. I was not paying attention and literally bounced off a student. He was a little over six feet and somewhat large for a ninth-grader. As a new student, he was ready for what he thought I would do and how to respond. However, my immediate reaction was to apologize and ask if he was okay. He did not know how to respond. I quickly said, "See ya!" and moved up the hall.

Over the next few weeks, I made sure there was a "hi" every time I saw him, and I made eye contact. (Incidentally, he was never a student in my classes.) About ten years later, I was in a restaurant, and I saw a familiar person sitting with a young woman and a small child. We made eye contact, and he lifted his hand to get my attention. He asked, "Weren't you a teacher when

I was in junior high?" I think he was surprised when I said, "Yes, I was. How are you, Eugene?" Point made!

2.10. GOOD LEADERS EMPHASIZE
THE CONTRIBUTION OF EVERYONE,
NO MATTER HOW SMALL

Research has shown that students know the difference between praise they earn and praise that is pro forma. Be careful of this. In working with students, it is necessary for all to feel that they are adding something to the situation. (And yes, you will have those who feel it is their role to not add positive ideas to a classroom.) In some cases, the teacher may have to set up the time and place for some to add to the discussion or activity, and this may not be the largest contribution. It may be a side comment. It may be a comment that adds comic relief to make all relax. (Make sure this does not become their only type of contribution.) But it is a contribution. Don't let it go by. Better to recognize something small that comes from a student than to give recognition just for the sake of recognition.

I was once in a class where, after a certain time, the teacher would rattle off three names: "Good job, Joey, Jane, and Juan." After another interval, there were three more names and a "good job." From my observation, these praises were wallpaper, things that the students did not even hear or recognize. Again, there is a balance between recognition, which is extremely necessary, and simply calling out, which the students know has little if any meaning.

3

About Your Teaching

3.1. GET OUT OF THE FRONT OF THE ROOM (GOTFOR)

You cannot reach students when you are trapped behind your desk or table or at the SmartBoard. Thoroughly plan to move about the room. If there is something on the board or SmartBoard that you wish to have the students write down, move around the room to monitor their work (and behavior). If a student is at the board, do not stand next to the student as if you are having a conversation with that student. Move away, and allow the other students to concentrate on that student's work. This is a perfect time to move around the room, especially to the back of the room, where problems usually arise.

This also applies when a student is presenting to the class. If you stand in front of the room, there is a chance that the students will focus more on you and your reactions rather than on the student's presentation. Also, if a student's explanation to a question is going to be lengthy, get away from the student so that you can ensure that the class is paying attention. Then, if a student is nonattentive, you can move to stand by the student or to a place where the student can see you. This might make the student feel uncomfortable (which could lead to a change in their actions).

Remember, in a good play, even if it is only a one-person performance, actors move around the stage. In a sense, getting out of the front of the room means getting out of the way because many times students focus on the teacher no matter what is happening.

3.2. TALK TO YOUR AUDIENCE, YOUR STUDENTS, NOT THE SMARTBOARD, CHALKBOARD, AND SO ON

In a discussion or in a presentation, eye contact is very important. When you are teaching, keep in mind that every time you turn to write something on a board, you lose eye contact. As a result, there is a pause in the communication between you and your students. Depending on how much you write on the board, this may give students an opportunity to set their own agenda instead of what they should be doing. Eventually this discontinuity leads to sporadic attention only when you are maintaining eye contact, and it is not conducive for a well-structured, continuous learning session.

If something needs to be placed on the board, do it before class and then refer to it. While the students are looking at it, you look at the students. After all, you know what is written on the board, so there is no reason for you to look at it. If you are going to read it, then read it from the back of the room. This will give you a view of what the students are doing as well as let you know if what is written is legible from a distance.

Good stage performers rarely turn their backs on the audience. When they do, it is only for a moment. When you watch a movie, see how often the lead actors have their backs to the camera. As the lead actor in your class, facing the students is of great importance.

3.3. PREPARE AS IF YOU OWN THE MATERIAL

Students do not want to know what the book tells them. They want to know what *you* want them to learn. As a result, your knowledge of your lesson plan cannot be left to what you write in your plan book. You must internalize the lesson so that it appears seamless (at least to the students). You may be constantly thinking about what you are doing, what comes next, and management, but you must look as if your work is as natural to you as if you were born doing it.

Just as a good actor seems to have no script and is speaking naturally about what is happening in the play, you should conduct your conversation with your students in a natural, comfortable way. Constantly referring to your lesson plans or to the textbook can have your students looking at you as the mere messenger. If this happens, you may begin to hear, "Why can't I just learn this on my own?" You know they will not be able to do this, but it does give them a way of taking the session off target. And telling them that they would not be able to learn it themselves sets up a confrontation of sorts about their ability to learn, and you do not want that.

Use reference materials for impact, not for direction. Keep your own direction, and make sure the students know it is yours.

3.4. GET TO TEACHING

Do not waste any time in class. Begin the learning process from minute 1, second 1, of the session. There will be some obstacles to this, sometimes from students, sometimes from administration. You may not be able to get away from these, but do not let yourself be the problem. When the time comes, begin to do what you love: assist students in learning. And remember, as in many other circumstances, the toughest thing about starting is actually starting.

If you want to have the students involved in the lesson from the beginning, have them do something associated with the focus of the lesson, in a sense a minilab. This is especially important for initial teaching lessons, when students have little knowledge about the topic to be addressed. It gives them a notion of what they are approaching. This acts as a vehicle, giving the students some incidental knowledge about the topic at hand, and it will help them realize where the lesson is going.

Beware of traditional or pro forma starting points, such as do-nows, which are reviews of previous material. These can be used if the ideas they address are developed in the previous day's lessons. If you need crowd control, the do-now can offer a system for having the students begin to focus on the work. However, if you can develop a readiness to learn in your students, the do-now can have all of you spending precious time on formality. If you spend 10 to 20 percent of your class time on a do-now (which could be as little as seven minutes), then you may not be able to cover 100 percent of your curriculum.

3.5. USE SIMPLE LANGUAGE AT FIRST; SAVE THE BIG WORDS FOR LATER

As an expert in your field, you can communicate to others in your field by using the technical, content-specific language. This is the language that has been developed by those in the field that allows others in the field to understand what is being discussed without a lot of introductory explanations. However, when someone is learning a subject for the first time (like your students), the technical language may interfere with addressing the conceptual ideas of the topic at the start. This does not mean that you are watering down the content. It means that you are using your deep knowledge of the content to use social language to explain the initial ideas to those who are trying to learn.

This calls for thoughtful planning on your part, but it is worth it. This gives your students an initial understanding of the content that will assist them when you introduce the technical terms and vocabulary. And remember, this is just to have the students discuss topics in the language they understand. As time goes on, they still have to become accustomed to using the more formal language of the content area, but this comes later, not at the beginning.

3.6. TEACH SIMILAR IDEAS AT DIFFERENT TIMES

People who deeply understand a content area can easily contrast and compare similar ideas. For example, biologists can discuss mitosis and miosis calmly without confusing the two. In mathematics, the mean, median, and mode are easily compared to draw conclusions from the data involved. Another example in mathematics is how students confuse the symbols < and >, which represent "is less than" and "is greater than" respectively. Although people who know mathematics or biology have no trouble dealing with these ideas at the same time, during initial learning that can be a problem. When people, like your students, are neophytes and just learning ideas, trying to address similar ideas at the same time can be confusing. Because they have not internalized the ideas, they constantly must focus on one idea and then the other. There is no way that, at the initial stages of learning, their thinking can flow from one idea to the other.

A difficulty in carrying out this teaching idea is that textbooks many times put similar ideas together. This is because the textbook is, in a sense, an encyclopedia of information on a topic, and therefore it is logical from a content standpoint to do this. However, instructional logic, which is based on how people learn, calls for the focus on one aspect of a concept so that learners have the time to internalize their understanding. Once this is done, they then have secure knowledge to address this concept in relation to others. This may call for creating a different sequence by which topics are addressed, especially if the course or subject is based on the contents of a textbook.

3.7. USE SHORT TANGENTS OFF A TOPIC
TO ADD INTERESTING IDEAS

Your zeal to teach your content is one of the reasons you became a teacher. You want others to know what you know. And hopefully, your teaching and their learning will allow them to enjoy the content as much as you do. However, do not let this zeal allow you to develop tunnel vision. Feel free to bring in discussions related to the content, even if they are not in the assigned curriculum. Such discussions make the content viable for many students and may be of particular interest to some students.

Such tangents could relate the content to a recent happening in the region or the world or to another subject that the students are studying. Linking these ideas is important to keeping your content alive in the students' minds. Obviously care needs to be taken that these tangents do not become the course. Use them as pressure releases, especially when the content becomes complex. There is a time when a break is needed.

3.8. USE TESTS TO ASSESS, NOT TO THREATEN

In this day and age, students know testing plays a significant role in the assessment of their knowledge. You must assess to find out what students have learned and to inform your teaching. However, students need to see assessments as ongoing occurrences and not have them posed as a threat. Statements like "If you don't pay attention, you will not pass the test" and "This is important because it is on the test" are not appropriate for motivation and can create anxiety where none is called for.

Students are not test anxious by nature. They are made that way by adults (either teachers or parents). Be better than that. Make sure your students know that learning is the important part of their education and assessments are a way for you to understand what they know so you can help them move on in their learning.

And it is really, really easy as a teacher to fall into the trap of reminding students that if they do not do or engage with the work, then the exams will be practically impossible for them. A former student of mine tries to avoid this by saying, "I think I'm a pretty smart person, but if you gave me a test in Russian right now, I would fail so bad, not because I'm dumb but because I didn't put in the work to study Russian." You must constantly remind them that the goal is to learn and, through this, be successful with assessments.

For this reason, goals for schools should be about learning and not assessment. Having a goal that "scores will increase by 10 percent" can be achieved in several ways, including largely relying on test prep. However, while test prep will help those who know the content by showing ways to answer questions, it will not help those who still do not know the content. For these students, test prep is a waste of time. Also, when students focus on test prep but do not do well on the assessment (because they never learned the material), they get frustrated. Assessments are road maps to get to a destination. They are the means to an end, not the end.

3.9. BE CREATIVE BUT MAKE SURE
IT LEADS TO LEARNING

Every teacher wants to be creative and have students learn. Notice there are two statements here. In being creative in your teaching, one of the important reflective questions you must ask yourself is, "How will this help my students learn what they should learn?" Merely having creative lessons does not foster learning; an objective must be tied to them. This does not mean that the students need to know what the lesson objective is, especially if they are enjoying the activity, but you should know. There is nothing wrong with students seeing what you wanted them to learn at the end of the lesson.

For example, if a person wants a toddler to take steps independently, the person moves away a few steps and holds an object the toddler wants. The toddler will try to walk toward the object. What is the toddler's objective? To get the object. Do they know that the person wants them to take some steps? No, and it is not necessary that they do (even if they could understand the idea). I once observed a class in which the teacher did not write the objective on the board at the beginning of class. At the end of class, she discussed what the students learned and then uncovered the objective that she had written behind the video screen before class.

3.10. WHEN IN DOUBT, USE COMMON SENSE

As happens to all teachers, there may be times when the lesson you planned is not going well. In these cases (as rare as you hope they will be), do not attempt to push through the lesson. Take a breath and ask yourself how to get your students involved in a discussion of what is going on.

If the problem in the lesson is the content, find out from them where they are having a problem. If the difficulty is class control, be honest with them and yourself, and try to discuss why they are taking the actions they are taking. It may be you, and it may not be. It may be something about which you are totally unaware. In this day and age, are their minds more outside of the classroom because of an incident than inside the classroom focusing on, say, Shakespeare? But in all cases, carrying on regardless does not work.

3.11. EVALUATE STANDARD PRACTICES BEFORE USING THEM

There are many classroom practices that are considered traditional or standard. Beware of them. Many were developed when educational practices were aimed at a much smaller segment of the population than today, with everyone learning in the same way. This has been a major reason the dropout rate in schools (both physical and psychological) remains high. The traditional practices that proved satisfactory for the brightest students in the past may not be the best practices for all students.

The problem we face is that nontraditional practices that work are not codified in teachers' minds the way traditional practices are. And schools of education or other training venues may not focus or even mention them, which makes sense. If you are reading this, then you more than likely are a college graduate. Do you realize the small group into which that puts you? Do you realize how many people your age never went to college, let alone graduated high school? Those are the people we need to reach, and the arms of traditional practice are just not that long. So there may be times when the typical discussion, experiment, or activity may not be your standard practice.

3.12. SEE YOUR LESSON PLAY OUT IN YOUR MIND'S EYE AS YOU REVIEW YOUR LESSON PLAN

Having a good lesson plan is necessary for having a good lesson. However, it is not sufficient. After you have completed the plan, read it slowly and attempt to visualize what will occur in your classroom at each step. Think about details, as well, such as

- Where will you be standing when a student is at the board?
- In what area of the room should you spend more time because disturbances seem to come from there?
- How much time should you allot students to copy notes that you want them to have?
- Are you using too many PowerPoint slides?
- Do you hear your voice too much?

Visualizing your teaching comes with experience in the classroom and takes practice. It is not like your dreams of being in a classroom as a teacher. Visualizing is a very focused activity that will improve as you gain experience as a planner and a teacher.

To help here, at some point, you may want to put your lesson plan aside and think about how the lesson will play out. See it, feel it, and touch it without the written outline. Once you do this, your lessons may begin to come to life. We have all seen people give speeches where they are reading from a page, with little eye contact with the audience. That is a speech, not a teaching and learning lesson. Create lessons not speeches.

3.13. DIVERGENT TEACHING CREATES DIVERGENT THINKING

According to Wikipedia, divergent thinking is a thought process or method to generate creative ideas by exploring many possible solutions. Teaching with such an idea eliminates plodding through the content to attain an objective. In many cases, especially in the upper grades, this is what students are expecting, having you stand there and tell them all the content you know. Some like this because they are good at absorbing the material. Others like it because there is no effort on their part. They just put in the time and take up the space.

Surprise them. Use your deep content knowledge to create unique ways of addressing the topics. If you diverge from the norm in helping the student address the content, your students may in fact follow with their own thinking. For example, instead of stating a rule for a mathematical idea, have students work with quantities in a real hands-on situation and then discuss the results and where they led. The divergent thinking used in the lesson can be helpful for students to reconstruct their knowledge in the future if there is a lapse of memory (like on a test). But they need to experience this type of thinking before they can internalize it and use it on an ongoing basis in their work. And keep in mind that remembering is a reconstruction of knowledge, not just a place in the brain where one goes to remember something.

3.14. AN ASSIGNED CURRICULUM MUST BE TAUGHT, BUT IT IS NOT THE ONLY PART OF YOUR STUDENTS' LEARNING

Addressing curriculum standards is one aspect of teaching. We teachers know that there is a curriculum that must be addressed. However, just hitting these markers is not the only part of the education that you give to your students. Knowing something and being able to think about it are not the same. I know that my car uses an automatic transmission. All I do is use a lever or button or dial to have the *D* show on the screen, and I am ready to move. I don't know how all that works (my father did), and really, I am not that interested in finding out.

When we teach, our job is not only to have the students know the concepts and skills they can use but also to understand them so they can be used in novel ways to develop more ideas. Another use of understanding is that if a concept or skill is momentarily forgotten (does this happen on assessments?), it can be reconstructed based on a deeper understanding, rather than just a surface understanding of the topic involved.

3.15. HIGH EXPECTATIONS BECOME A SELF-FULFILLING PROPHECY FOR YOU

You have heard many times that we have high expectations for our students, and we do expect them to attain them. But this leaves you with the responsibility of setting high expectations in your teaching through your lesson planning and your lesson delivery. You see, expecting something from someone is a two-way street. If the expectations are high for our students, then we must give them high-quality support. Holding yourself responsible to make your teaching creative means developing lessons that are an amalgam of the ideas you research and the synthesizing you do to mold them into your own lesson. When this is a starting point, students know that you have done your part. Does this leave a better chance that they may do theirs? Maybe yes, maybe no. But you have tried your best to do your part.

3.16. SWEAT THE SMALL STUFF. DON'T LET IT BECOME LARGE

As your days go on, you will notice that students will become more comfortable with you. This will lead to occasional discussions and kidding around. It is fine to have informal, casual discussions with students. However, do not let these off-topic discussions consistently carry over into your teaching. If they do, address them right away. Letting some small incident go by without action could leave the impression that this is permissible. For students, they need to know your boundaries with this.

Some students will feel that, because it is okay on occasion, they will only do it occasionally. However, with twenty to thirty students in a classroom each doing or saying something funny occasionally could take an entire period to hear and address. Yes, you have to address it. It might be small the first time one student does it. It will be large (and time consuming) when several students start this. So when it occurs the first time in a lesson, say calmly that it is something you would rather not have occur. Be careful of being too heavy-handed by using such statements as "inappropriate" and "is not allowed." Save these for more important issues.

If students ignore you, then that raises the level of impact, but it is their responsibility and not an issue that you allowed someone else to do. The typical response you do not want to hear from a student is, "But Jonathan said something funny, and you didn't do anything about it." This is where the trouble truly begins.

Humor can be an essential element to keeping the classroom real. However, students need to know there are limits, and it is your responsibility to set them.

3.17. INCREASE THE COMPLEXITY OF THE CONTENT, NOT THE DIFFICULTY

For the most part, an expert in a content area can easily make the subject difficult for someone trying to learn. When we look at our own backgrounds, there may have been instructors who showed that their subject was easy to make difficult. With all due respect, I believe mathematics is one of the easiest subjects to make difficult, but it can happen with others.

In your teaching, as you develop the content, you need to move the students deeper. You have to help your students accept the challenge of addressing complex ideas, but you must do this without discouraging them by just making it difficult. What you need to find is the right level at which students can work with complex ideas before the work flows into the world of difficult.

At the beginning, you may want to look at difficulty in two ways. First is the quantity of material. Reading three novels may not increase the complexity of the content, but it certainly increases the difficulty. Adding numbers in the millions may not add to the complexity of mathematics but it certainly adds to the difficulty.

A second way of looking at difficulty is language. As stated earlier, addressing a subject or a topic within a subject should begin with a language structure that the students can understand. Imposing a more intricate language structure before the students can deal with it makes the learning more difficult but not more complex.

3.18. YOUR TEACHING CANNOT MAKE YOUR STUDENTS LEARN, BUT IT CAN CREATE LEARNING

You will have some students who almost say to you, "I dare you to make me learn." I think every teacher has had or will have such a student. But the idea is that you cannot make students learn. Your responsibility is to bring the ideas of the subject in such a way that students may think it is interesting. This obviously does not happen with a PowerPoint lecture or a whole bunch of similar worksheets. Also, it does not happen by assuming that they know something from last year. It comes from your creative use of your deep knowledge of content and your ability to share and listen to other professionals with similar ideas. Teaching effectively to create learning is a joint venture, bringing together professionals at many levels. Yes, you cannot make them learn, but you can be ready to make their learning a good possibility.

3.19. TEACH IT RIGHT THE FIRST TIME (TIRFT)

When it comes to getting your students enthused about a topic, you have, in a sense, one bite at the apple. A lively introduction, no matter how most may look at the topic, is necessary to get the students to decide that it is worth paying attention to. And the responsibility for this is yours. As a result, more than any other lesson, the initial lesson on a topic is the most important. Developing this takes time, thought, and research. The key element here is to make sure the lesson addresses the topic in a way that your students will be able to understand and accept.

Also, teaching it right the first time means that you will not have to do the most difficult thing. This is when a topic is not initially taught well and students develop incorrect ideas, and you must have your students unlearn what they know before they can approach it correctly. And that undertaking takes more time than you have. So TIRFT! And save your students a lot of time and effort.

3.20. PLANNING: BEWARE THE "SUNDAY PANIC"

So you go into school on Friday, determined to use time at the end of the day to begin planning for Monday. But before you begin, colleagues come by and announce a Friday get-together to relax after a tough week. You promise yourself that you will join them and wake up early on Saturday to begin your planning, so you go.

You wake up Saturday afternoon only because you were so tired from the long school week, but you cannot plan now. You have things scheduled, and you must do them. But you know you will do your planning early Sunday, so you can really think about it.

On Sunday, family and friends intrude in such an uplifting way that your good intentions are sidetracked. As the day goes on, you bask in their good energy. Until the bewitching hour, which, in this case, may be around 6:00 p.m. And your inner voice says, "You still have to plan for tomorrow!" And so, in a near-panic situation, you begin to plan with the foremost intention of getting some type of plan done.

Many teachers have gotten caught in this situation, and I believe they will tell you that creativity in planning is almost nonexistent. With such pressure to get it done, you know your mind cannot relax enough to be creative. So be careful in your planning. Make sure you give yourself time to create a different approach to the content and not just a repetition of what is in a textbook or direct instruction to have students successfully complete a worksheet. But also consider attending some of those Friday get-togethers. They refresh you.

3.21. BEWARE OF DEATH BY POWERPOINT (DBPP)

A videographer once told me that Microsoft Word was a word-processing program in which you could display graphics and PowerPoint was a graphics program in which you could display text. However, PowerPoint has become a constant display for text. Many times, people use a presentation program to show outline after outline or, worse, paragraph after paragraph.

The use of PowerPoint calls for a passive, note-taking audience. In a school classroom, this may be a good idea for a few minutes to set the stage for the lesson, but that's it. Using this wonderful tool more than that invites a lack of interest on the part of the students and slow but sure disengagement. Like any tool, technological or whatever, it must be used to keep the students interested and engaged. When the tool becomes the focus of the lesson, the students suffer. And when students suffer, they may pass the suffering onto you.

One thought on this: Taking notes does not create learning unless the notes are read. Most times in a college class, we took notes and studied them after class to discover what the instructor was talking about. There was little if any learning in the class itself. Most students you have in school are not like this. Oh, yes, they will take notes if you require them to do so, but many will not then take them and study to learn. In a school setting, learning happens in the classroom.

3.22. REACH FOR YOUR STUDENTS (TEILHARD)

Jesuit philosopher and mystic Teilhard de Chardin once said something like,

a. When we teach, we push our knowledge back to its simple elements,
b. For the audience of our teaching does not have equal footing with us.
c. We must go back and raise them to our level.
d. In this, we must seek to begin the process with the simplest ideas of the topic.

Some thoughts on "a" to "d":

a. This is about our planning. How do we take our knowledge and create learning situations in which our understanding is in its simplest form?
b. We may miss this simple idea. Students are in our classrooms because they do not know what we wish to teach them. They may know nothing about what they need to learn.
c. This focuses on beginning where they are and moving forward. Some may say, "I need to begin here in order to address all the standards," but beginning "here" may automatically require the ability to learn from some of your students. Where to begin? You are the teacher, so you need to create a way of having your students meet the content at some mutually agreeable point to begin moving forward.
d. During the initial teaching lesson, when the students first address the content, they must see it as something doable, understandable, and something they can learn. And, as said previously, it must begin with simplicity.

3.23. UNDERSTAND THAT YOU HAVE BECOME A DEDICATED LIFELONG LEARNER (DL³)

Teaching is both an art and a science. As we know, art and science are two fields that change over time. Sometimes there are exciting breakthroughs, and sometimes there are periods of consolidating breakthroughs. As a teacher, you are signing up for a life of breakthroughs and consolidations.

No matter what time frame you are in, new learning in both content and pedagogy is constant. That is what you have become: a dedicated lifelong learner. Just like we tell students that they must be lifelong learners, we teachers must constantly study our fields, from both a content and a pedagogical standpoint, to make sure that we are using the best ways to assist our students in their learning.

You will find times when you may not want to discuss other ideas. You may feel that what is happening is just fine. Beware (and that is the best word here!). You have an obligation to investigate such ideas to make sure that the decisions you make are best for your students. Keep in mind that teaching is not about you. Ignoring new ideas is the start of you becoming a teacher whom all of us promise not to be when we enter teaching: those who teach the first year over and over again. Again, someone with whom I worked for many years said, "There are those teachers with twenty-five years of experience and those who teach the first year twenty-five times." Choose wisely and continue to learn throughout your life. Become a DL^3!

3.24. DON'T LET THE LONELINESS OF BEING A CLASSROOM TEACHER GET TO YOU

As a classroom teacher, you are never alone. The students are always with you. (This may contradict the title for this section, but please read on.) However, teaching is one of the few professions in which you may not see other adults on an ongoing basis during the day. Please keep this in mind as you enter the profession. As you continue your career, this will become clear.

The camaraderie you felt with peers in your previous life experiences and during your time away from the classroom will not be matched as a classroom teacher, and you must be aware and prepared for this. As a classroom teacher, you can defend yourself against this by not getting into a groove that has you going through the same scenario each day. You do not have to change your whole procedural manner, but just do something different every once in a while. This may be something simple, like beginning the class with a discussion of how the present topic fits into the overall course or a discussion of something that happened in all your lives, both good and not so good. This change in routine may not substitute for another adult presence, but it may help to keep you fresh (at least for a short time until you need it again).

The teaching profession is one of the few professions in which you cannot simply go get a cup of tea when you want or just step outside and take a breath. Everything has to be planned, so take some opportunities to unplan it.

3.25. BE CAREFUL OF "SAME STUFF, DIFFERENT DAY" THINKING

In teaching, your schedule is very important to you, as it is to the students. The human mind craves routines, and when it comes to the classroom, for the sake of harmony, routines are important. Yet routines do not mean the "same stuff, different day" mentality.

As a teacher, you must use your creativity and knowledge of your subjects and group dynamics to take your classroom on different journeys throughout the year. This may mean beginning class with a discussion away from a content issue. (It gives your students the idea that your subject is part of and not exclusive from the school community. What goes on in the school affects your classroom.) This may happen in your class after a school assembly on a topic of high interest to your students. In this case, educating your students is more important than covering your content curriculum.

You may need to learn and practice activities before you do them in your classroom. This is the homework for teachers, the gathering of things to do in the classroom that were never done in classrooms when you were a student. You might have students lead a lesson. Yes, you give them time to prepare and help as much as you can. They might understand what you do so much better when they walk for a few minutes in your shoes.

3.26. DATA ARE IMPORTANT. MAKE SURE IT IS SIGNIFICANT

Schools, like many organizations, have taken the technology for efficiency and created "do it by the steps" routines as they strive for data-driven information. The importance of reviewing data cannot be overlooked. However, the data collected must make sense and have meaning. Results on tests do not matter if the tests are not focused on what is communicated and learned. So although difficult, when called upon for data, make sure that the information you submit can be used well.

Now this sounds like something where you immediately say, "Of course," but be careful. Over the 180 days (or more) of a school year, this collection may become so routine that you feel you just have to give them something. And this, you have to admit, is not what you signed up to become. So keep in mind that, while data are important, you are the only one who can make your data valid and significant.

3.27. DON'T FOLLOW THE BOOK.
IT IS AN ENCYCLOPEDIA

We begin with a question: How do you have a person become interested in something? We all know that encyclopedias contain vast amounts of knowledge on a particular topic. The entries are written by experts who have spent years studying the field and can explain it using the proper vocabulary in the field. So it is with textbooks. From the beginning, they are masterful works demonstrating the content to be studied as well as the author's knowledge of that content. And therein lies the difficulty.

Many times, textbooks portray the topic in a format that is logical for an expert. The difficulty is that the audience of a textbook is not a group of experts. Most students are using textbooks because they do not know the content. (Before you continue here, you may want to read section 3.22 on Teilhard.)

Textbooks are an instructional guide. While they portray the subject matter, they do not necessarily portray the content in a sequence in which a learner can address it, and they may not use the wording that the learner can understand. (Words in bold in a textbook usually cannot be used well at first because most of these words are new to the learners.) You as the teacher are the great interpreter of the text. As an interpreter, you must add context and nuance so that the content is brought to a level in which the learner can begin to acquire the knowledge, so somewhere down the road, the learners can read the text and understand it. Putting ideas in a logical format only comes after one knows the ideas well enough. Sometimes in learning a topic, it may be best to initially forgo the logical sequence until the students have internalized the ideas and have acquired the true meaning of them.

3.28. IF YOU KNOW, SAY SO. IF YOU DON'T
KNOW, SAY SO AND FIND OUT IF NEEDED

While working with people, especially children, there are questions, and when you are asked a question, there are two important ideas. The first is, obviously, do you know the answer? However, the real issue as a teacher is, should you know the answer? We are all ignorant on some topics. How nuclear fusion works comes to mind. But if you are asked a question you do not know the answer to, then you need to say, "No, but I will find out and let you know," or some type of phrase depending on the age of the questioner. And if you try to be cute and tell the student, "That is a great question. Why don't you find the answer?" you will find the number of questions diminishing over time.

To the second point, what does it mean when you are asked a question that you should know the answer to because you are the teacher of a subject? The response comes in two parts. First, you must find the answer. But second, and maybe as a wake-up call, you may be starting to lean too much on your prior knowledge of content and not keeping aware of what is presently going on. This relates back to section 3.3, about owning the material, and section 3.23, about becoming a dedicated lifelong learner (DL^3). Yes, this takes work. But life changes, the world changes, and your knowledge must also change, sometimes letting ideas go and finding new ideas.

3.29. DON'T LET THE DETAILS GET AWAY

Big ideas are very important to developing a great plan for any endeavor. But of equal importance are the details that allow you to implement your plan. Make sure you know them as an integral part of carrying out your plan. All too often, it may be the small things that bring the big ideas down. When you plan, insert the important details into the plan. Possibly use a different color typeface or a different font for this. While you teach, the big idea will always be there. The details may be the things that get away:

For want of a nail, the shoe was lost.

For want of a shoe, the horse was lost.

For want of a horse, the rider was lost.

For want of a rider, the message was lost.

For want of a message, the battle was lost.

For want of a battle, the war was lost.

For want of a war, the kingdom fell.

And all for the want of a nail. (thirteenth-century proverb)

3.30. EXECUTE YOUR PLAN, EXECUTE YOUR PLAN, EXECUTE YOUR PLAN!

Writing a lesson plan is a great *start* to having a successful lesson. This idea is fully emphasized in your teacher training program. It is important to have a great plan. However, implementing and executing the plan is what creates the learning experience for the students. Although this seems like a no-brainer, many times the lack of good execution is the main reason your lesson does not go well. So if you have a great starter for the lesson, get to it. Start the class as you planned. Don't wing it. If you wander through the class time until you find something to do, you may lose the students to their other activities. According to Tom Peters, a famous corporate consultant, execution of a plan is the all-important last 95 percent of your work.

3.31. IF YOU ARE NOT FOCUSED, THEN YOUR STUDENTS WILL NOT BE EITHER

There is a joke: "The speaker spoke for thirty minutes. At that time, you could see in his eyes that he had finally hit on something to say." As a teacher, you basically plan four to five hourly events for each day, five days each week. And if you teach middle or high school, you may not have to plan four or five hourly events each day, but you may have to repeat the same event four or five times each day.

(Note: A principal told a first-year colleague he was giving him a break. He scheduled him for five Algebra I classes. At first, the teacher was elated, envisioning planning for one class each day. As the year went on, he saw his incorrect thinking. At the beginning of the year, it became boring repeating himself five times a day. He yearned for something different. As the year went on and assemblies, fire drills, and half-day sessions took hold, he found himself keeping very copious notes for each class because none of the classes were ever at the same point in the course.)

The challenge of being focused in a classroom is huge. First, for the teacher, the content is somewhat basic, even in an advanced class. (Even advanced classes are nowhere near what you studied in your undergraduate years.) So the challenge is to maintain focus and teach as if this was really exciting to you, even though you have known the ideas for years. Do not become the absent-minded professor who roams around with thoughts and then begins to speak. The model you present to your students is the model they will possibly replicate. (Yes, you are always in danger of being replicated!)

3.32. LANGUAGE, LANGUAGE, LANGUAGE

Oral language is a very important part of the teaching and learning process. However, remember: The teacher's command and use of the language in the classroom is usually far superior to that of the students. This is true for both the academic language as well as social language in casual conversation. When it is obvious that the students cannot put the words together to explain what they mean, ask them to create a way of demonstrating their ideas. This could be using physical materials or visual devices. In doing this, the student is freed of the constraints of academic language, of which, at this point in the learning process, they do not have mastery. This allows the student to begin to add language to their answer once they see the whole idea in front of them instead of trying to attach proper language to each level of an explanation.

3.33. INVITE THEM INTO YOUR CLASSROOM

Students enter a classroom using all styles of behavior. Some bounce in, ready to go; others seem as if they are being dragged in by some mystic force (usually called their schedule). No matter, be a conscious host. No, you don't have to thank them for coming, as if they had a choice and chose you. Nor do you have to act as if this is a red-carpet event. However, don't make them feel that you have more important things to do, like getting the attendance ready (you know, bureaucratic stuff). Make sure they know that you are glad that they are there. (After all, if they weren't, you would be in a different job.) Sometimes the details of teaching get in the way of this. One way to avoid this is to set up your materials for the day at the beginning of the day.

Some schools require students to line up outside the door, and as each enters, the teacher shakes their hand and welcomes them. Now for you and your school, this may be a little over the top, but somewhere between this and ignoring them until the bell rings, there is a proper format for you to acknowledge their presence before the formality of class.

4

About Your Students

4.1. DISCIPLINE IS PERSONAL. KEEP IT THAT WAY

A main objective of the entire educational experience is to teach self-discipline. Self-discipline comes in many varieties. There is the self-discipline to focus on a task. There is the self-discipline to listen carefully to what someone says. There is the self-discipline to not interfere with another person's work. These are all learned by each individual. What this also means is that you do not discipline the entire class. Such actions make discipline impersonal and punitive. Although an interpretation of discipline is something punitive (we discipline a student), the type of discipline necessary for learning needs to come from within.

In the same way, when a student needs to be spoken to, do it one to one. Commenting to a student from across the room (unless it is an emergency) must be avoided. Reason: It creates a show of you and the student, which is encouraged by the audience (the rest of the class). If you need to speak to someone during class, move about the room and then casually speak to that student (review section 3.1 on GOTFOR). And plan to do this. Just don't rush to a place and create attention. Make it part of the way the class flows.

4.2. PRAISE IS IMPORTANT WHEN IT IS DESERVED

Letting students know that you appreciate good effort is very important. Do not be shy about telling them. You can use the language comfortable to you and them, depending on their relationship with you. For some students, it might be "Great job." For others it might be a "Nicely done." And for others, it might simply be a nod.

But be careful of being a praise machine. This is when praise is strewn around the room like water out of a hose: "Nice job, Joe, Pat, and Kelvin." "Thanks for paying attention, Livia and Estella." (This one is sometimes used to tell others in the class that they need to pay attention. It is not about Livia and Estella as it is as much a statement to the class.) After a while, all this praise becomes background noise to the students. They don't hear it and don't pay attention to it. And if the praise is for something that they know they have not done well, they will see through the facade. Let them know they are doing well when they do well, and let them know often. But be careful because students, especially older students, are wise enough to know when it is not sincere.

4.3. STUDENTS EXPECT AN ADULT
FOR THEIR TEACHER: BE ONE

Being friendly to the students is extremely important to gain their confidence and have them become successful learners. However, there is a difference between being friendly and being a friend. The former is necessary. The latter has too many downsides to implement. Students do not expect to see you to be one of the group. They need to see you as someone in charge of the class (kindly, of course) and who will guide learning, the reason you are all in the school.

Your demeanor and dress should establish and foster that relationship. While you may not dress in business attire, you should portray a person who is carrying out the duties of their profession. This means not wearing clothes you would wear to weed the garden or fix the car. Present thinking about being "with the students" may make the idea of good demeanor seem old fashioned. However, it is mentioned here so that you know that you do have this option. Look at the teachers who truly have the respect of students (and this means more than just being liked) and those who do not. From that, make your decisions about how you present yourself.

4.4. DON'T TAKE IT PERSONALLY: THEY
ARE NOT LIKE THAT

A majority of the students you meet will be fine. They will have their moments, but by and large, they will try to cooperate (although they will need direction). However, there will be a small group of others. When you deal with them, remember that how they treat you is many times the way they treat others, so don't take it personally. This will be difficult. When you are dealing with their constant interruptions, it is hard not to take it as a personal affront. This is where you need to be more of an adult than most people are asked to be at any time in their lives. (The only exception to this are first responders, who are asked to be the adult, no matter the situation.)

To deal with this, visit another class and observe these students in a different environment. There are two reasons for this. First, you can see if they are the same in other classes. Also, it may make them wonder why you are there, which can be helpful in the future. The goal is to create a connection to resolve their inappropriate behavior. Sometimes you can, and sometimes, unfortunately, you will not.

4.5. BE AWARE OF THEIR WORLD OUTSIDE THE CLASSROOM

Emotions have a great impact on a student's learning. As we teach, we must be aware of aspects of the student's life outside the classroom that may affect their ability to focus. Above all else, students want to be safe. We teachers want to add two other aspects to that: Namely, we want them to be happy and educated.

However, a student's life outside school may not make them feel safe in school. Some students, while sitting in your classroom, are still thinking about what they have been through so far in the day and what awaits them after school. We know we cannot control this. However, we cannot discount this and act as if it does not exist or does not make a difference because, to the students, it does. So when students do not seem to be trying to learn or are pushing back against your dedicated work to have them learn, keep in mind there may be circumstances that neither you nor they can control, and you must do your best to find out what this is. This does not excuse you from attempting to get them to learn, nor does it excuse them for misbehavior of any kind. However, it must be on your mind as you make decisions dealing with them.

4.6. DON'T ASSUME THEY LOVE YOUR SUBJECT AS MUCH AS YOU DO

For many of us, our love of our subject is a wonderful study of ideas and skills. For many students, there is a fear and trepidation in some subjects that we cannot understand. Where does this come from? It could be their prior experience with teachers who knew the content but were unable to explain it clearly enough for them to learn it.

It could also be a handed-down oral history from friends and siblings, including "Ms. Avila is really hard," "Spanish is impossible," and "Wait until you get to the trig functions." While we do not know why students fear the unknown (no pun intended for you math people), they are prone to fear failure.

With this in mind, there are some things we can do. By the second or third day of school, all your students must believe that they can be successful. This means that, in the first days of class, you must create lessons that show what they will learn as a learnable. Lots of vocabulary and technical terms, as well as a review of learned concepts and skills, is just not the answer here, especially if they know that their school experience to date has not been good.

Also, throughout the year, when introducing new material, make sure that the students are involved in lessons. If you are going to (or have to) use a do-now, make it something that leads into the lesson. This could be a lab-type activity, a game, or the use of physical models. As the students move through the initial activity, tie it to the lesson's objective, making students active participants and using their own work to create enthusiasm for the ideas.

4.7. IN A PEER GROUP, MAKING MISTAKES MAY NOT BE A LEARNING MOMENT

Teachers, teacher educators, and professional development leaders all speak of learning through mistakes. The line usually goes something like this: "Don't be afraid to make a mistake. We learn from our mistakes." And then the prophets of this idea are asked a question in a group discussion with their peers. The silence is palpable. No one responds. Personally, I have seen this when I have taken classes. In meetings, I sometimes find myself avoiding responses. So as part of the development of the class climate, teachers need to develop the idea of learning from mistakes. Simply going in and telling the students that making mistakes is a way of learning is not in sync with their experience in the past, where making mistakes have led to failure on a test, a poor reaction from an adult, or criticism from peers. So be careful. Getting students to think and then attempt something is the essential idea behind "Mistakes are a learning opportunity." But it, like most learning skills, must be nurtured.

And then there is the idea of making a mistake in your peer group. This is one area in which almost all people are hesitant. It is one thing for teachers to ask their students to try and then learn from their mistakes. It is another for teachers to take the same chance in a graduate course, professional development setting, or school meeting. Sometimes, teachers respond in their own peer group in the same way that students in their classrooms respond in their peer group.

4.8. STAY POSITIVE EVEN WHEN FRUSTRATED. REMEMBER, THERE WILL BE TIMES WHEN THEY ARE FRUSTRATED

There will be times when you plan an excellent lesson, you have all your materials in order, the students are ready and then (a) a fire drill, (b) an announcement over the speaker system, (c) a visitor with a message from the principal or a colleague, or (d) the technology does not work as it should. And then sometimes such lessons begin slowly for these reasons and unravel.

The frustration you feel is normal. Things did not go as planned, and now you find yourself trying to catch up. Keep in mind, teaching is a human activity filled with the joys and frustrations involved in anything humans do. Do not let this or any other frustrations become overwhelming. Face them and then decide how to get around them. Don't let giving into frustration become part of your mantra.

On the other side of the desk, when you have taught a spectacular lesson with no interruptions, when all has gone well, there may be frustration for those also involved (or maybe not so involved) in the lesson. Student frustration sometimes comes quickly. They could think, "I am not smart enough," "I am not good at this," or "I don't have the brain for this." And sometimes, this is before you begin the lesson. The students have not seen the material and have already made the decision to be frustrated. The problem is that their frustration is contagious and possibly moves to other students and even to you. Students not learning what you are trying to teach is immensely frustrating for them.

This is why you must keep your frustration in check. No matter how difficult it is, stay positive and vocalize this to your students. The real difficulty in this situation is that, in their minds, they are allowed to vent their frustration, and you cannot. Does this call for superhuman strength? I am not sure, but it certainly calls for a steady mind and the knowledge that this is all part of the teaching and learning process (as painful as that may sound).

4.9. ASK FOR AN OBJECTIVE VIEW OF YOUR INTERACTION WITH A STUDENT

"What is wrong? Why do we constantly have a conflict?" young Kate asked herself about her inability to connect with a student. So she asked a colleague whom she trusted to observe her class and relate to her what he saw. After about ten minutes, the colleague asked to speak with her: "Your demeanor, your stance, the language of your entire body tells him you are in conflict with him. It is not as much what you say as your demeanor when you say it."

Kate thought about this. Then she tried to be more objective with herself and began with a simple realization. She, a petite 5′3″ woman, was dealing with a 6′2″ young man. Just that alone, she realized, was enough to put her in a defensive mode, especially because she was in charge (she hoped). Was this rational on her part? Who knows? It was not the idea of being rational as much as it was dealing with the objective reality. And that, for anyone, is not easy to do when you are trying to be objective about your own outlook. But remember, you cannot be objective about the way you interact with people because your whole being, your ego, and your emotions are tied up in the interaction. It may be wise to ask for someone else's view of the situation.

4.10. THEIR LEARNING IS MORE IMPORTANT THAN YOUR TEACHING (SO WHO SHOULD BE CENTER STAGE?)

While affected by the art and science of your teaching, student learning is different. For teaching, the instructor is the center of the work. However, for learning, the learner must be at the forefront. In teaching, we must remember that, no matter what the teacher does, no matter what research-based ideas they bring into a classroom, and no matter the artfulness with which they present the material, if there is no consideration to the way the students learn, it is all for naught.

As a teacher plans a lesson, thought must be given to how the students will first discover the content, how they will be motivated to take it as their own, and how it can be absorbed into long-term memory. These three ideas must inform and drive the teacher in the preparation of a lesson. And you must remember that, even if you are teaching the same content to different students (either during the same day or in different years), how you approach one group with content may not fit well with another group.

And, yes, this is what planning entails. Although the format of the lessons might be the same, what happens as the plan unfolds in different classrooms or with diverse groups may be different. But no matter: Because the student is the focus of the work in schools, they need to be center stage (or pretty close to it).

4.11. ARE THEY LISTENING AND LEARNING WHEN YOU DO NOT KNOW IT? WHAT ARE THEY LEARNING WHEN THIS OCCURS?

Students in a classroom are different from an audience at a play. First, the students not only see the performance of the teacher, but they also see the teacher in reality. Students see the teacher in the classroom, prepared to have them learn the content so they can be successful in school.

However, the students also see the teacher in reality: that is, before and after the planned lesson, out of the context of the classroom, and in some cases out of the atmosphere of the school. Whether adults like it or not, young people watch how the adult acts and maybe look for guidance on how to act as they get older. Teachers must be aware that students see them in many contexts in a school day, from the classroom to the hallways, before, during, and after school, so whether they like it or not, examples of life and living are always present in the teachers' demeanor, speech, and actions, both inside and outside of the classroom. You would not give your students poor information in your classes, and the same holds true when they see you as a person outside the classroom.

4.12. THEY SHOULD NEVER BE SEEN AS "THESE KIDS"

The students who walk into your classroom are the students who walk into your classroom. It sounds funny, but it is true. What happens from that point on is up to how you and they work together. For most, what has happened before in other classes and with other teachers may be the baggage they bring with them. And it is also the baggage with which you will have to work. Notice, what was said: *with which you will have to work*, not *with which you will have to deal*. Dealing with students is a negative. It promotes the idea that they are who they are at the beginning of the year (which is true) and this will not change (which is not true—it is based on how you work with them).

A September episode:

TEACHER 1 (walking into the faculty room): These kids in ninth grade are much more immature than last year's ninth-graders.

TEACHER 2: Do you mean last year's ninth-graders in June or last year's ninth-graders last September? I really cannot recall what last year's ninth-graders were like in September.

TEACHER 1: leaves the faculty room.

In all walks of life, you will find people who wish to make judgments at the beginning, as if they are omniscient. You are going to have to work (not *deal*) with such colleagues. That is the life in a community.

However, you cannot allow such statements to influence your work. Don't ignore such statements, but question both their validity and reliability. The answer to this question can only take place in your classroom. You must beware of statements that begin with "These kids." They usually are followed by a negative tone that does not do anyone any good. Let students tell you who they are and what they are about.

4.13. THEY ARE WHO THEY ARE

At the end of my first year of teaching, I was told by a colleague, "Wait until you get Stillwell next year." As it happens, the next year came. Stillwell walked past me into my classroom, and I kept looking for the 6'2", 200-pound ninth-grader that I was sure Stillwell would be. When it was time to begin class, I counted heads (twenty-six students) and the names on my roster (twenty-six students). So Stillwell was there. I called the roll, and when I said, "Stillwell," a young man, maybe 5'5", answered.

There are those in any walk of life whose judgments border on the far end on the frustration scale, and they just love to share their frustration with you. Again, this is when you hear about "this kid" or "these kids." Yes, I must admit I was cautious of the immaturity of those ninth-graders, as well as Stillwell, so many years ago, but I never gave it credibility based on the opinion of another.

4.14. BE AWARE OF THEIR PROJECTS
OUTSIDE YOUR CLASSROOM

Students complete all types of projects as part of their school experience. Depending on grade level and the school, there could be a large number of projects that are not part of your class. No matter when these occur, it is good for you to show an interest in what they are doing. This may mean simply discussing a school event or project with your supervisor or a colleague to gather information. Even if you do not fully understand it, many students could be very excited to discuss their work, and it may surprise them that you are interested. This may even call for you to show up. This could range from an art expo to a battle of the bands. Be that as it may, it is important to show that you are definitely interested in not only how they do your work but also their other endeavors.

On a more important level, if the child does not have the support from caretakers, your interest may enthuse them to keep going on the project and possibly do a better job with it. It may seem simple (and some might even call it trite), but for many students, it is a great investment of your time in their lives. In the future, they may not remember that great lesson when you showed them how to solve a quadratic equation or the deep analysis of the required play. But they will remember that you showed up.

5

About the Content

5.1. KNOW IT, KNOW IT, KNOW IT

You are a content specialist whether you teach one subject or many. This is especially true when you compare your knowledge of a subject to that of your students. Knowing content is a necessary condition for teaching.

The deeper you know your content, the more creative you can be in the classroom. Deep knowledge of your subject allows you to be able to see a topic from various perspectives. This is your gateway to creative approaches in your classroom. Obviously, this means that merely knowing what you want the students to learn is not enough. You cannot be a creative teacher by staying one chapter ahead of the students.

This may mean that you have homework to do. You need to keep in touch with the content you teach and the methods of teaching it. Remember, you are a DL[3] (see section 3.23). Don't forget this and let your students down.

5.2. LEARN AND PRACTICE HOW TO DISCUSS CONTENT WITHOUT TECHNICAL VOCABULARY

When we begin to learn something new, we need to clear it in our own minds before we can begin to speak about it. In this clearing, we use our own words to develop true meaning on our own terms. So as a teacher, you must train yourself to initially discuss new content using simple, nontechnical terms. And you must know the content well enough to be able to substitute such terms into the discussion. This allows students to focus on what is going on without constantly referring overtly to the meaning of words. Once they understand the concepts and skills involved, then the vocabulary can be introduced. In this way, the students are able to substitute a formal term for a simple one when it concerns ideas they already know. Again, Teilhard!

5.3. NEVER LET THE CONTENT GET BETWEEN YOU AND YOUR STUDENTS

You love most, if not all, of the subjects you teach. If you teach elementary children, you may not enjoy social studies, but you will teach it. If you teach high school English, you may love African literature, but you will still teach British literature. You are a true advocate for the content.

That's great, but be careful. When students come to you with problems, remember that they are more important than the subject or the tests that they take. You know the pressure you and your students are under to cover content and the associated assessments. However, the students and their needs come first.

This does not mean that you should not care about the content or the assessments. However, do not disregard what a student may be going through in their personal or academic life. Be aware and be ready to act on these. Although you cannot sacrifice content, people really do come first.

5.4. CREATIVITY COMES FROM A DEEP KNOWLEDGE OF CONTENT

What makes one creative is a deep understanding of what they know and the ability to put these ideas together. This calls not only for deep content knowledge but also its applications to other school subjects and the world at large. This is why lifelong learning is important to a teacher (DL[3]!). The world changes. Maybe a lot of the subjects you teach do not change (certainly reading and arithmetic seem to be immutable). But the way you approach subjects, the way you put your students in touch with it, and the way you constantly try to picture it in different contexts keep you always on the verge of having a creative breakthrough.

However, some creative connections may be great in your mind but just don't fit the situation in your classroom. That is okay. Know your students and their level of development to choose the creative leaps in which they can join you and be excited about and which are more likely to confuse or frustrate. There will be missteps in deciding between the two, but in time and through a solid knowledge of your content, you will know more instinctively which connections to make and when.

5.5. KNOW YOUR CONTENT WELL ENOUGH
TO RELATE IT TO THE STUDENTS' WORLD

School programs should relate content to the students' world. The question that must be raised is, What is the world of our students? For this, there is no national answer. There is no one world in which all our students live. Students in a rural northeastern area have a world different from students living in an urban midwestern area.

You want your programs related to your students' world. You have a great deal to do with this. Developing a program related to your students' world calls for two specific things. First, you must get to know what their world is about. What are their interests? What do they think is great? What do they think is lame? After this, you must take your deep knowledge of content and find those topics that can creatively bring this knowledge together with the students' world. Easy? Not really. Necessary? Absolutely.

5.6. Take Their Misunderstandings as That, Not as an Unwillingness to Learn

Did you ever sit in a classroom where you really wanted to learn but unfortunately did not really understand what was going on? If this has happened to you, then, as a teacher, you have an experience that some of your students may have. They do not understand. It is not that they do not want to learn or do not want to understand or cannot understand.

Remember that there may be those in a classroom who consider school a waste of their time. Students with this type of immature thinking are not who I am addressing here. I am talking about those students who wish to learn, but no matter how good you think the lesson is, they are not going to understand. For you, this may be frustrating. (Certainly, it will be for the students.) As the saying goes, you do not understand why they don't understand. And that is true, but you need to find out.

Discussions with the students may be one way of finding this out. Taking the work apart one step (or even one half-step) at a time, though time consuming (and frustrating for you), may be the way to go. But just keep in mind that, for the most part, students wish to learn. They just do not understand, and as the teacher, it is your role to bring understanding to them. You cannot make them understand. You have to bring them to understand.

5.7. EXPLAIN YOUR EXPERIENCES (GOOD AND BAD) WITH THE CONTENT

Students sometimes see teachers as content experts but think that teachers do not understand what it is like to have difficulties with learning. As you move through the content, you may want the students to know that there were times when you had a rocky time in your studies. From this, you can discuss productive persistence and productive struggle.

Productive struggle occurs when the content does not come easy. This means that you needed to struggle with the topic, possibly go over it a few times, and even have someone else help. Relate that this is something almost everyone goes through. Even people who are considered excellent may have some productive struggle when they learn new content and need to get their ideas together and in order.

Productive persistence, though, is when there may not be difficulty with the work; it is just a matter of getting it done. For example, you may understand an idea very well. However, even though you can see how to apply it in a novel way, you may need to take the time to just get it done. And sometimes that can be boring. (I offer as an example rereading your own writing several times before you submit it.) It is like taking an exam where, after you read the exam, you know that you will be able to answer the questions well. However, now you have to sit there and do that. It is not a struggle to answer the questions, but it is a matter of productive persistence to answer the questions and make sure that, in your haste to finish, you do not leave any important ideas out.

5.8. DON'T MAKE CONTENT THE BE-ALL. THERE ARE OTHER THINGS IN LIFE

You as a teacher are hired to teach, so for the most part, this is what school administration expects. But how it is done depends on you, your way of thinking, and how you deal with people and your content. As a teacher, you cannot see the people you teach and your content as one monolith. A teacher must bring the content together with the students. You cannot give it to them. You must make it acceptable to them.

But this means having them fit it into their lives. In this case, you are entering an area, their lives, about which you know very little, if anything at all. So if you make the content the be-all, students may ask, "Is this all there is? Am I going to be here each day and just deal with this?"

In a school year, there are times when content has to take a backseat to the reality of school life. An assembly on race relations cannot be forgotten when the students come to a class where you are planning to discuss the 4 times table or the map of Europe or the significance of *King Lear*. It is at these times when the students need you to focus on them, what they have seen, what they are seeing, and its impact on their lives.

Case in point: After an assembly on race relations, my seventh-graders came into the room. It was obvious that their heads were still in the assembly, so I asked, "What is going on?" And out it came. As the discussion began, my principal walked into the room for an observation. I took a breath and continued the discussion. It lasted the full period, and he stayed for the full period. When the bell rang, I dismissed the class. I saw him walk toward the door. Was I worried about him not seeing a mathematics lesson? You bet I was. As he reached the door, he turned and simply said, "Nice job." Without another comment, he left.

There is no moral to this encounter, just that's what happened. Before you analyze the dynamic between my principal and me, think about my students as they left the room. My math lesson could wait. The reality in their lives could not.

6

About Your Supervisors

6.1. BEGIN WITH THE IDEA THAT THEY WANT TO HELP YOU. LET THEM PROVE OTHERWISE

There are two major jobs as a supervisor: The first is to make sure things are going well, and the second is to make sure everyone is doing their best. The key to all this is the first. The first job of a supervisor is to have things go well. So when you are visited by a supervisor, keep this in mind. They want to know what you are doing, why you are doing it, and evidence that it is helping your students learn. Don't hold this against them. Their job is to ask for and seek information. Good supervisors are not being intrusive; they are simply doing their job.

Sometimes, however, you may meet a supervisor who wishes for you to follow their directives, no matter what is happening in your classroom. They may think this is the best way to get their job done and really do not consider you or your ideas. In this case, they are not doing their job correctly. They have gone against the job they should be doing. If this ever becomes the case, be careful, tread lightly, and maybe consider a teaching position in another school.

6.2. REMEMBER, IT IS EASIER FOR THEM IF YOU ARE A GOOD TEACHER

Good supervisors love good teachers and are able to identify them. Supervisors love good and excellent teachers for several reasons. One is that the supervisor knows that the students (for whom they are also responsible) are being given the direction and assistance they need to learn. Also, on a more selfish level, supervisors love excellent and good teachers because the interactions with them are positive. The only stress with such interactions is finding the energy and time to continue to support these teachers. Good and excellent teachers give supervisors the positive feedback they need to continue to do what is right.

This job, while difficult and challenging, is much easier for the supervisor than if a teacher is not good. Determining why a teacher is not effective, convincing such a teacher that this is the case, and then providing ongoing remedial assistance, while worthwhile, is not a supervisor's first choice. The supervisor's job is much more enjoyable if they are working with good teachers. However, they need to address poor teaching. It is not their choice but their obligation.

6.3. LISTEN TO THEM CAREFULLY WHEN THEY GIVE YOU SUGGESTIONS

A discussion with a supervisor can be informal. However, when you are new to teaching, you should consider it a formal discussion, no matter the attitude of the supervisor. Listen to the supervisor carefully, especially when they give you suggestions. They can be just that: an idea that you may want to try. However, think seriously as to whether it may help your teaching (see section 6.2). If you do try the idea, make sure to give the supervisor feedback, whether it worked well or not. If it did not go well, ask for a meeting to discuss what occurred. Assume that you did everything correctly, even though this may not be the case. Again, listen carefully. After this, determine on your own whether the idea was good or not. You are responsible for what happens in your classroom, no matter who says (or suggests) what.

One more idea: Ask the supervisor to return to your classroom the following week to review how you are modeling the asked-for changes. Such a request shows that you care about your practice and your supervisor's feedback. This also helps you know if the changes you have made were the ones being asked for and if they are having the desired effect on your classroom. The sooner you can fix a problem, the better. The more proactive you are in your work, the happier your administration.

6.4. THINK CAREFULLY BEFORE YOU FOLLOW THEIR SUGGESTIONS. THEY MAY OR MAY NOT FIT YOU WELL

Any suggestions about your teaching should be considered carefully. However, unless they are mandated (and yes, this may happen), you should think about a suggestion and its fit for you as a teacher. This is not to say you should reject it outright, especially in your first years of teaching. However, you should work it into a style that permits you to be you as a teacher. Unless you are really not doing well as a teacher, consider all suggestions in light of what you see as your role in teaching. This is important so that you can maintain yourself as a teacher and not try to become someone else (which you will not be able to do anyway).

For guidance on this, carefully look to your students and gauge their reaction to the change. If you see them take to it, then you may want to consider the change as part of your arsenal of instructional ideas. If they do not, then this should be a topic in the follow-up discussion with the supervisor who made the suggestion.

6.5. ALWAYS BE PREPARED TO EXPLAIN YOURSELF IMMEDIATELY WHEN ASKED (AND WITHOUT NOTES!)

College courses are a marvelous compilation of knowledge, notes, and references. Being able to speak on a topic at length without notes is not stressed in these experiences. As a professional teacher, things really change. You may be challenged on how you approach a topic. You may be challenged by the way you deal with class management, homework, parents, administrators (shall I go on?). Your first response in any of these situations is very important, and in many cases, your response must be immediate and to the point.

When people say, "As a teacher, you must know what you are doing" (and I agree with that), you must know as yourself, not as an academic. You must not only truly understand what you are doing but you also must be able to verbalize this to someone who may question it, whether that be another teacher, a principal, or a parent. Certainly, principals and parents deserve to know if you know why you are doing something with students whom they have put in your care.

Being conscious of your practice means not only being able to teach but also being able to explain to others (administrators, parents, other teachers) why you made certain choices in creating and delivering a lesson and creating an environment in your classroom. Being able to explain your thought process should be automatic. If it requires time to think about your moves, then you need to spend more time in planning and preparation of your moves.

6.6. BE DIPLOMATIC AT ALL TIMES

As in any human endeavor, there are going to be times in your teaching career when you will want to say exactly what you think. Best advice: Don't! Being diplomatic when you want to tell someone off shows more personal skills than when you are just being cordial in a social situation. And remember that what you say when heated cannot be undone. (When it comes to oral language, there is no undoing; there are no inverses.) So whether you are being given the utmost compliment or whether you are being told that things are not going well, respond in a way that will keep things moving along.

In the case of a commendation or award, false humility shows, so accept it with grace (and with total glee in your heart!). One of my colleagues was once told, "I hear you are a great teacher." Her response: "That's what they tell me."

In a negative situation, stick to the issue and not the personalities of those involved. Make sure your points are known and that your side of the story is heard. Do not use statements about the lack of knowledge of the other person, although you might mention if certain facts are missing from their statement. While both basically say the same thing, the former refers to the person, which is not good. The latter is about the issue, a much better place to be.

Lastly, being diplomatic does not mean being run over because you cannot be honest. Being honest is part of diplomacy. It is in the way it is portrayed. Do not be treated unfairly or dishonestly without a response (whether from you or a representative). But even then, keep it civil. This will not be your last teaching position, unless you show yourself as being unreasonable despite the obvious (the obvious is that something is not going well). Know and exercise your rights! But be diplomatic.

6.7. STAY POSITIVE EVEN WHEN FRUSTRATED. REMEMBER, THERE CAN BE TIMES WHEN THEY ARE FRUSTRATED

All people get frustrated at times. You will see this as you move through the year. You may not be able to tell the context of your frustration or that it is coming. When dealing with supervisors, frustration may come with you thinking they do not truly understand what you want to do. Or it may be that their direction does not fit into your style. This can cause frustration.

What it may come down to is first giving them the benefit of the doubt. Their lack of understanding may not have anything to do with you. In fact, what you may see is their frustration, not with you, but with something else.

They may not even know it. They may think that they are hiding it from you and trying to deal with you in a professional manner. Unfortunately, most of us are not good actors with hiding our frustration. Even when something is working well, our frustration with something else may seep into whatever we are doing.

As stated earlier, *first* give them the benefit of the doubt. In a short time, speak with them, and try to ascertain if the issue was you or something else. Hopefully it is the latter. However, if such an attitude on their part continues, then it must be addressed (but with diplomacy and not with frustration).

6.8. RESPOND WHEN THERE IS A PROBLEM, BUT DON'T ANSWER BACK. STAY PROFESSIONAL IN RESPONDING, NO MATTER HOW HARD IT IS

As part of a school community, problems will arise. This is a natural course in human events. As a teacher, if you are involved, you must respond. If the problem has to do with your teaching or your classroom or with an activity you are conducting outside the classroom (club, group, etc.), you need to be the responsible adult and address it.

In working with your supervisors, no matter how they react (whether slowly with understanding or quickly as if on the attack), hold back on the quick, adolescent-type retort. Don't answer back as a reflex. In responding to the problem, maintain your demeanor as an adult and as a professional. Keep both. Don't have one without the other. Although this may be difficult, make sure that there is at least one person in the room acting like an adult and a professional. And let that "at least one person" be you.

Whether the administration views you as the cause or you as the one who let it get out of hand, clearly state your position. Accept the responsibility that is truly yours (if it is), but do not accept any more than you should. Let others step forward and accept their share. This is the only way the problem will be solved.

6.9. IF THEY RAISE A PROBLEM, TAKE IT SERIOUSLY BUT NOT PERSONALLY

When dealing with the school structure, problems occur. They may take the form of student behavior, student academic focus, or your teaching. No matter the problem, make sure that you ascertain the serious nature of the problem to the school community. What you should never do is take the problem personally. It is not you as a person that the problem is about. It is about the situation and your relationship to it. It has not happened just to create a problem for you. It has happened because things happen. As I say in the title of this section, take it seriously but not personally.

However, with anything that happens, you must defend yourself. This is where you take it personally. Sounds contradictory, but not really. It is about balancing your role in the problem and your role in solving it.

6.10. ASK THEM TO DEMONSTRATE WHAT THEY ARE TELLING YOU TO DO

In the course of your work, supervisors will offer advice on how, in their view, you can improve your teaching and the students' learning. There will be times when the advice is in line with what you do, and you will be able to address and implement it. However, there may be times when the suggestions are something you either do not understand or do not feel will fit into your work. At these times, you have the absolute right to ask your supervisor to come to your classroom and demonstrate with your students what they are suggesting.

If your supervisor works with your class on the idea, then this is helpful in that you can sit in the back of your room and objectively view how your students are reacting to the work. Also, it gives you and your supervisor a common ground, your classroom, to continue discussions about your work and the implementation of the curriculum.

However, be alert to those supervisors who will make suggestions but will not demonstrate them to you. This may mean one of two things: First, it may mean that they are making pro forma suggestions (just to make a suggestion) and are not truly serious that it will make a difference. Far more problematic is when the supervisor refuses or declines to demonstrate the idea because they do not have the expertise to do so. If they expect you to do something and you ask for assistance, then they need to provide it. A caveat is that they provide someone else who will come and work with your students. However, in this case, the supervisor should also be at this lesson, again giving both of you common ground for later discussion.

It may not be beneficial to have the supervisor send you to another teacher to see something. While this might be helpful, the demonstration is not with your students and does not consider the dynamics of your classroom.

6.11. INVITE THEM INTO YOUR CLASSROOM

There will be times when your classroom is humming and what you have planned has taken hold and things are going well. (This may not seem possible in your first weeks of teaching, but it will occur.) This is a good time to share the wealth. Explain to your supervisor what is happening and invite them to visit and observe what your students are doing. This will have two results. First, your supervisor will understand that you are attempting to do a good job and that you are trying to be creative. You will be seen as someone who can join the conversation of having the grade and school make progress. Second, the observation happens on your terms. Many times, teachers who are told that they will be observed attempt to create a lesson to showcase what they are doing. Normally, supervisors can see through this, and though they may give a good assessment, they may not think that this is the best use of their time.

What you offer with your invitation is the opportunity for your supervisor to see your classroom as it is, as you conduct it on a normal basis without any bells and whistles that are the cornerstone of a showcase. It makes your work seem natural to your supervisor giving the sense that you are capable of continuing with it.

6.12. DON'T SURPRISE THEM. LET THEM KNOW WHAT YOU ARE DOING, ESPECIALLY SOMETHING CREATIVE

In teaching, you want to begin simply with your students and then lead them to something significant. If this happens when you are being observed by your supervisor, it may be a good idea not to surprise your supervisor. Give them enough information about what you are doing to have them see the connection of the initial teaching lesson to the main idea. The important part of this is to show them how you move the students through the lesson and how well the students make the connection. If your observer knows where you wish to go, then they have a better view of how you are doing it by seeing the incremental movement to the objective.

Now, they may not agree with the direction the lesson takes to achieve the major objective, but this brings up the issue of style, not content. If you achieve the objective, then how one arrives there is a matter of professional judgment: that is, either yours or the supervisor's. Giving them the opportunity to think about what you are doing by providing a "road map" before the lesson will give them time to think about your approach and accept it.

Surprising them, especially as a newer teacher, may leave the supervisor wondering if it really is going to help in reaching the overall objective.

6.13. MAKE IT A POINT TO TALK TO THEM REGULARLY; DON'T MAKE IT A POINT TO AVOID THEM

There is sometimes a tendency for teachers to avoid supervisors. You have to make a judgment about whether it is possible to approach them. (The attitude in the faculty room may be one of avoidance.) One of the things you do not want is to make it a habit of avoiding supervisors.

They will know you as a teacher when they visit your classroom, when they see the results of your teaching in your students and their results, and when your work is discussed at administrative meetings. But you also want to let them know what kind of person you are, that you have a personality and can carry on a conversation about something other than teaching or schools. However, this must be authentic on your part. Do not get into the habit of seeking them out and constantly asking for their assistance or commending them on their work. This will do more to make you look weak and like you don't have what it takes to be an excellent teacher. Yes, like most important things in your career, there is a balance. Make sure you do not lean too far in one direction.

6.14. SHARE YOUR STUDENTS' SUCCESSES

Supervisors in schools are looking for widespread success. This is what makes a school strong. Having strong success in social studies but not in mathematics (or vice versa) is worrisome for school leaders. They are responsible for the success of students across the board. They may not have the time or the view to see successes at a smaller level, such as in the classroom. Sharing your students' success can support their work in two ways. First, good news is always appreciated. Hearing the success of students is always a great experience for supervisors. The major issue is that, if you do not tell them of successes, they may not be able to see the trees because they are paying too much attention to the forest (the whole school). Second, for them finding a hidden success story may provide information that helps on a broader scale. Being successful with students while others are as well tells them you are keeping up.

However, your success may be in an area in which the school is not doing well. Your information may give ideas about how to solve some situations that have been problematic until now. So do not be afraid of mentioning it. Don't belabor the point, act the hero, or engage in any type of theatrics. Tell them, and let it sink in. You never know. Your success story may lead to a directional change for wider success. If improvement is the goal, then your work may be considered, and you may become part of the problem solvers the school can depend on. Creating the persona of dependability is an excellent way to have your ideas heard and maybe even considered.

6.15. SAY NO IF SOMETHING IS NOT A GOOD IDEA (CHAPIN'S GRANDFATHER AGAIN!)

In a school year, there are a huge number of ideas that people develop in many areas, whether focused on the classroom, student movement between classes, systems for school dismissal, and more. As a teacher, you will be responsible for implementing any idea put in place. But if you do not feel an idea is good, you need to say so. This does not mean giving a grand speech against the motion in a school debate. Just point out in simple yet focused terms why you do not think the implementation would solve the problem, and then be ready to offer an alternative. (It is said that, when one approaches a supervisor with a problem, they should also have a solution in hand.) Not doing so and letting it go by may put you in a poor position later and one that many will not know about.

Reread section 1.4 on being tired. What you don't want to do is fight the battles of others, especially when you had a chance to show a different perspective. Being left with a poor group decision on which you did not comment leaves you in a position of not being "good tired." And yes, disagreeing with peers and supervisors may have consequences, but so does just going along. In fact, it may be that just going along begins the road to burnout. While identity with a group is preserved, your own identity may be taking a hit, which is not good. You want to try your best to be "good tired."

7

About Other Teachers

7.1. FIND PEOPLE WHO KNOW WHAT THEY ARE DOING

One of the best things you can do for yourself is to find other teachers who know how to teach, how to deal with students, and how to conduct themselves as adults in the school. The obvious question is, How do I find such people? Well, they will not be wearing signs, but they will be giving signs. One idea for you is to ask other teachers if you can visit their classes while they teach. When you do this, the important thing to watch for is how the teacher interacts with students. It is from this that you can begin to build a list of those colleagues who are worth visiting again (and again!). Also, be polite. If you realize right away that the teacher is not for you, don't just up and leave. Stay for the period, thank them for their time, and leave it at that. (Your time is limited. Use it to visit good teachers.)

When you find a colleague you feel can help, ask for another visit. If possible, engage them in informal conversations when the time arises. And maybe, if you feel comfortable doing so, ask them to discuss with you a problem you are having in your teaching. Good mentors are waiting to be asked. Do them a great favor and ask them for assistance. But be careful of running to a mentor with every problem. Sometimes, try to solve it yourself and then discuss it with them. Make sure they know that they are helping you, not giving you all the directions you need. They want to help, not manage your classroom. They have their own to think about.

7.2. HELP COMES IN MANY FORMS
(FORMAL AND INFORMAL)

Many schools assign a veteran teacher to act as a mentor for a new teacher, so as a new teacher, you might have a colleague to talk to and discuss your classroom work. But there are others who can help. As you move through the school, look for those colleagues you find others going to. It may be another new teacher who tells you how great their mentor is. This may be a person to put on your "get to know" list.

As time goes on in your career, there is a tendency to do things your way. This isn't necessarily bad, but you don't know if it is. It certainly is comfortable for you. Why not link with a colleague to discuss each other's classroom work? Why not open up to areas that year in and year out drive you crazy? Remember, the ideas about teaching being a lonely job (see section 3.24)? Finding a colleague to discuss your work with means you will have another voice to assist you in making your year of teaching the best it can be.

7.3. COLLABORATE ABOUT STUDENTS
YOU CANNOT REACH

This may be something you do not want to admit, but you may come upon a student (or students) you cannot reach no matter what you do. Instead of taking the brunt of their opposition (whether active or passive), try to discuss them with other teachers who also have them in class. You may find that this is the beginning of resolving the problem. (Also, you may think you are the only one who cannot deal with such students. It is good to know that there may be other teachers facing the same dilemma.)

If you find a colleague who has mastered the skills of working with these students, ask if you can visit their class when these students are present. Don't be surprised by the reaction of the students when they see you in the room. If they ask what you are doing there, tell them that you are interested in the topic that the teacher is covering (even if it is not in your field—nothing like being a renaissance person).

Watch carefully for what works and what does not and how your colleague's approach differs from yours. Keep in mind your colleague may do things you feel are not you as a teacher. That is a decision for you: accept that you cannot do something they've done or think about doing it through the fine art of acting like it is you. Be careful, though. Students are excellent at knowing when you are not being you, and they will call you on it. The main goal here is to find a way to reach students so that they will be successful, not docile in your class. This sounds great, but it takes work to have it happen.

7.4. BEWARE OF COMPLAINTS THAT BEGIN WITH "THESE KIDS" (REDUX)

You will meet many personalities in the profession. These people will come with outlooks based on their view of teaching and their experiences. At some point in time, all will have a complaint about students. It is a natural phenomenon. But beware those who talk about "these kids" (see section 4.12 to review this idea).

And you will hear it no matter where you teach. In what may be termed good schools, you will hear about the indulged student. In not-so-good schools, you will hear about the undisciplined student. It will always be that the student has too much of something or too little. Remember, while the student is a large factor in their own success in school, so are you (see Fulghum in the preface). And your mindset, whether overt or covert, will make a difference.

7.5. TALK TO COLLEAGUES ABOUT BEST WRONG ANSWERS (BWAS)

The faculty room is a huge venting area. It is where teachers feel free to let go of their frustrations from the day, the week, the month, the year. At times, this is necessary. We all need to let it out at some point. However, there will come a time when you wish this would stop. The negativity strewn about by some keeps the conversation away from things that can help you in your classroom and the entire school community.

Instead, you can begin a discussion about best wrong answers (BWAs). Students' incorrect responses are always a frustration for teachers, and sometimes teachers wonder how a student really got that answer. So why not begin a BWA board? All you do is post a wrong answer with the question, "What happened here?" It can lead to some interesting discussions as well as help teachers to make some headway in dealing with these students. And this may be humorous when colleagues respond, "No clue at all" (NCAA, as one colleague put it), or "It must have been in a parallel universe." But it gets the conversation started. And remember, the toughest thing about starting anything is starting!

7.6. LET WHAT YOUR STUDENTS LEARN
TELL OTHERS ABOUT YOU

You will hear some colleagues extolling their teaching prowess, how things they do always go well, and so on. For yourself, wait until your students begin to influence other classes. If you are effective, then good colleagues will begin to see a difference in your students as the years go on. This is especially true with teachers who also have your students in their classes.

Will they run up to you and compliment you for your work? I doubt it. But there will be comments under the radar. You will need to listen carefully. Or it just may be a bigger hello than usual later in the year. But don't be surprised if the comment is, "Sure, they work for you. You're young and like all the stuff that they love." Remember there always will be people who are masters at the backhanded compliment, especially when it means that they may have to change something in their monolithic teaching style.

7.7. MAKE FRIENDS WITH SOME;
MAKE ALL YOUR COLLEAGUES

When you begin teaching, you are joining a group of adults who work with children or adolescents. This common endeavor brings you in touch with many types of people. As with your outside life, you will be involved with people whose personalities fit your way of thinking. Some of these people may become your mentors, and some may become your friends.

However, there will also be others whose personalities do not fit your way of thinking. Unlike your life outside school (except for family), your freedom of choice is limited. While these people may not be the type to be your friends, as part of the school community, they must be considered colleagues. They must be seen as part of the work of the school community. You may be teaching children they also teach, so communication is essential. And although these people need not become your friends, you must maintain a working relationship with them because the objective of giving your students a good education depends on all the adults working together.

7.8. DON'T LET YOUR SILENCE BE
TAKEN AS AGREEMENT

In a community of people, there are many issues, all of which lie on a spectrum from "very important" to "not so important." As a member of the community, you may be asked to be part of the conversation. While at times you may feel this is not the best use of your time, you still must fulfill your obligation. No matter where the endeavor lies on your spectrum, you must maintain a level of involvement that does not portray you as agreeing just because you are there.

For example, someone in the group begins to use terminology like, "It seems natural that we all agree with. . . ." Be careful here. While you may not be asked to express your opinion at that time, you may hear your name used later by the part of the group seeking to have something done. So a rule of thumb is to voice your opinion. If you agree, say so. And if you don't agree, make your thoughts known. Again, this does not have to be argumentative but thoughtfully stating the reasons for your position.

It is important that, as the decision is disseminated to the whole community, members know your position. Even if all do not, you can clearly bring it forth later without the smaller group seeing you as changing your mind. Letting people know your ideas on an issue is necessary for you to maintain your integrity and not just being seen as a cog in the wheel.

7.9. IF A PROBLEM ARISES, BE AN ADULT

In any community of people, problems arise. In schools, they can involve students, other teachers, the administration, parents, and more. This is going to happen. How you address such things is up to you.

One idea you must hold on to is that, whatever the problem, you approach it as an adult. While this may seem trite, it is not. People in organizations sometimes act as immaturely as children or adolescents when they do not get their way or their lead is not followed. Do not fall into this trap. If something needs to be addressed, address it. If you need to have a discussion with someone, do so. Do not avoid addressing people, but avoid confrontation. It leads nowhere.

Keep the needed composure. Sometimes this will be difficult, especially when people get angry at you for not seeing how logical their position is. Remember, you cannot yell your way out of a situation. You must keep your integrity and your composure. You lose these when you yell. Mark Twain once commented that, when you argue with a fool, those watching the argument may not be able to tell the difference.

7.10. HELP WHEN YOU CAN, NOT
WHEN IT IS CONVENIENT

There is never enough time. You know this just from the life you have lived, no matter how old you are. And yet, in a school community, there will be times when others need help with either a project or an event. As many times as possible, offer to help, not just when you have the time. There will be circumstances where you should make the time to help. If someone is giving their own time, then you should be willing to rearrange some of your time to give assistance. It is not just being a good member of the school community but also being a good colleague.

And when your assistance is offered, make it seem a natural time to do it—no stories about what you are giving up or who you have to call to postpone something else. Just be there without the drama so you do not make the person you are helping feel indebted. That is what real help is all about.

7.11. SOCIALIZING IS GREAT IF YOU WANT TO

In any organization, socializing with colleagues is a great way to relieve the pressures of the job and get to know other people. This is especially true in teaching. As said earlier, teaching can be a lonely job because you are with children (no matter their age) all day. While in other professions, the formal job-related interaction may lead to colleagues knowing who each other is, with teaching, there may be people in your school you will not see from one week or month to another. So when the call goes out that an adult social event is happening, consider it strongly.

However, as with everything else, there may be times when it does not fit into your schedule. You have your own life to lead outside school, so sometimes being a nonattendee may be a necessity (see section 3.20 about the Sunday panic). It is important that you are the director of the balance you need.

7.12. BE HUMBLE BUT AFFIRMATIVE

In any situation, you want to give everyone a chance to be part of the group, so you must give people space to express their ideas. Sometimes, you may need to be a little humble and allow others to speak. This is especially true in dealing with people who normally do not participate or have shown themselves reluctant to express their ideas (and this could be a group of people with excellent ideas). However, continue to be affirmative in your ideas, even if there is disagreement. There is no use in allowing ideas to which you cannot subscribe. Continue to listen, yet continue to make your points.

As has been mentioned many times, there is a balance. Be careful of false humility when someone expresses a not-so-good idea and you feel that interjecting your knowledge may be too much. This may not be the case. Don't make that kind of decision until you have expressed your ideas in the discussion.

Don't be humble to the point where others think you do not have an idea or points to make. This is unfair to you and your reputation, which you must protect at all times. However, as you make your points, do not let your knowledge be the only force. Overplaying your expertise can overwhelm people and cause the discussion to shut down or become a monologue. Remember, there may be people in the group who have good ideas but not your expertise. Do not be the cause of their ideas not being expressed.

8

About Parents and Caregivers

8.1. PARENTS AND CAREGIVERS ARE SENDING YOU THE BEST CHILD THEY HAVE

In a keynote address to New York City teachers several years ago, my colleague Dr. Bob Gyles said that teachers had to remember that parents send their best children to us to be educated. He did not say that they sent children who are necessarily good at learning or very personable, but they are the best children that the parents can send. Keep this in mind when you are teaching. Wherever they are, your students are someone's child, and they deserve your attention. Even when they react negatively, your patience must be there.

And before you form judgments, contact the parents or caregivers. If no progress is made, then is the time to begin to get the school community involved. But do not do this before you let the parents or caregivers know how well their best is doing. Keep in mind that the overall message is "Do for the student."

8.2. PARENTS AND CAREGIVERS MAKE GREAT PARTNERS IF YOU ASK THEM

Never put yourself in a position where a parent or caregiver can say, "But no one told me." Yes, it is difficult to call someone and discuss a problem their child is having. Yes, they are going to be defensive. Don't forget, the only information they may have gotten is from your student. And with all due respect, information from a child or adolescent may not be 100 percent accurate.

So be proactive. Contact parents or caregivers when you need help, and surprise them by contacting them when things are going well. You will be surprised how shocked they are. It is very rare (what are the odds of winning a multimillion-dollar lottery?) when parents or caregivers of a problematic student will contact you, so you have to ask them. Having parents or caregivers as partners can be an excellent tool for the student's success, but be specific. Don't let the conversation ramble on to topics you feel will not help the student. If the parent or caregiver goes there, listen supportively and then bring the conversation back to the issue.

Parents and caregivers can be great partners in helping you help a child, but you have to approach them and offer to do your part. Their joining the partnership may be just what is needed for the student.

8.3. SOMETIMES VOLUNTEERING IS NOT IN A PARENT'S OR CAREGIVER'S DNA

Parents and caregivers have a lot to offer you as a teacher. Their backgrounds, experiences, and lives can enhance what you want your students to learn. And they know things about your students that you will never be able to learn from a school interaction. However, there are many parents and caregivers who are not forthcoming about what they can offer because they never think that they have something to offer. (Yes, I know, for the cynics among experienced teachers, there are some parents and caregivers who think they are better teachers than you are and know exactly what their children need, but let's not spend time on this very small minority.)

Approach parents or caregivers, adult to adult, when they least expect it. By this I mean when there is no issue in the classroom, maybe just an email asking for volunteers to create learning centers. (You provide the idea, structure, and materials. You are asking for people to put the materials together. Having some coffee, tea, or soft drinks and snacks for them would not hurt.) Then, once they are in the classroom, the discussions begin about future undertakings. Don't jump into a discussion about them being a chaperone on a field trip. You need to ease into that one over time.

Case in point: Years before hands-on math materials were readily available, a principal asked parents to volunteer for a project. Over two days, the parents and caregivers cut strips and squares, and by the end of the project, every student in the school had their own set of base-10 materials. Did their work solve the problems of the year? No. But it opened a link between those parents and caregivers and the teachers who would be using the materials. They had accomplished a small but vital project. Possibly the next question was, What else could they be helpful with?

Meeting parents and caregivers when there is not an issue takes time, but it is well worth the effort so that if an issue does arise, you are seen as a person they know, not through the interpretation of their children. And as you should know from your own schooling, a student's view of the teacher can be somewhat biased. Remember, they are children, no matter how old they are.

8.4. PARENTS AND CAREGIVERS KNOW A DIFFERENT SIDE OF YOUR STUDENTS

Because of frustration, not impatience, you might say to a parent or caregiver, "I cannot understand why Frank. . . ." This begins a defensive stance on the part of the parent or caregiver. You are seeking information from the person who knows your student a lot better than you do and possibly hears about what goes on in your class from them. This discussion may have the parent or caregiver thinking about the situation, not reacting to a "This is what he does, and I want it stopped" statement.

Also, such a conversation needs to remove the parent's or caregiver's total deniability (except in extreme cases). You are portraying objectively how the parent or caregiver understands your interactions with a student. For them, it is not easy to be objective about someone to whom they have devoted so much time and who is facing a problem. Listen intently to their responses. Try with all your energy to glean information that will help you help their child to succeed. This information may or may not be there, but you have to listen for it. And you never know: A few days later, the parent or caregiver may send information to you after they have had time to understand who you are and your objective of helping their child.

8.5. SOMETIMES PARENTS AND CAREGIVERS ARE INCORRECT. HOW DO YOU RESPOND?

Diplomacy is not a big topic in teacher training, but as a classroom teacher, it is one of your greatest assets when dealing with students, supervisors, and administrators. However, it is a basic skill that is truly needed when dealing with parents and caregivers. Most times, the parent or caregiver is the dominant advocate for their child, and that is the way it should be. Of course, when the student is incorrect and, based on the information they give, the parent or caregiver is also incorrect, the situation becomes delicate. (By the way, there may be times when your student finesses what they say to the parent or caregiver, which may not align with the facts.)

When a parent or caregiver approaches you about an issue, and it is obvious that they have the wrong information, the first thing you want to do is hear them out. Let them tell you all that they know. (Being interrupted when they are making a case raises the level of the confrontation, and you obviously want to avoid that.) Let them know that you are glad they made the appointment to see you, but make sure that this does not come out as you immediately wanting to tell your side of the story. You are there to discuss the actions of the student, and that is what is most important (no matter how thin your patience may be with the student—and the parent or caregiver—involved). As they speak, make mental notes of inaccuracies. When you respond, begin with your whole story about what is going on. Make sure that you touch upon the areas that they have either interpreted inaccurately or the incorrect information they were given.

There are going to be situations where you will need to have a supervisor or principal sit in on the meeting. This should not be done to show your power but to have an arbiter to keep the discussion positive.

8.6. CONTACT PARENTS AND CAREGIVERS FOR GOOD REASONS

Surprises are always nice, and nothing surprises a parent or caregiver more than when their child's teacher contacts them out of the blue to relate a positive note. As with many things in life, we are quick to focus on the negative things that happen because we wish to correct them. For example, when a supervisor speaks to us, no matter what they say, we are always waiting for the world-famous *But*. So no matter how well or poorly a student is doing in class, when something positive happens that you feel is noteworthy, make it known, certainly to the student, as well as the parents or caregivers. An email from your *school* (not personal email) can do this.

A note of caution: Make sure your intentions are authentic. Make sure the parents and caregivers understand that what you are relating is noteworthy. Don't come across as giving them something that will hopefully have the student move on a different path. This is for other, more formal discussions. For these incidental contacts, give the parents and caregivers something to enjoy in the moment.

8.7. DON'T GET BETWEEN YOUR STUDENT AND THE PARENTS OR CAREGIVERS

Conflicts with adults are a natural consequence of the changes children go through and how their view of the world is developing. As a teacher, you will certainly see this. These same children will also have disagreements with their parents or caregivers. It is natural, and it happens to everyone, including us.

If they bring this conflict to you, as a teacher, you are at best a listener. Be supportive of your students. They are the ones with whom you have a relationship. However, when dealing with a student–parent issue, do not under any circumstances take sides. Be the greatest listener you can be. Be the greatest support person you can be. But do not let your judgments be known to the student.

If you feel something is amiss, that the parent–child relationship needs assistance, contact school personnel who have more training than you do in this area. But here again, you must be careful because you may not feel that the school personnel are the best to help the problem. You may speak instead to adults you have come to trust about the problem the student has. This could possibly be a teacher who also has the student in their class.

You want to have these issues resolved because they are not good for your students, but you must maintain your role as a listener. Make sure you steer the situation to those who have experience and can truly help.

8.8. BE ALERT THAT NOT ALL PARENTS AND CAREGIVERS DO THINGS IN THE CHILD'S BEST INTEREST, NO MATTER THEIR STATUS

While you should not take sides in a conflict between parents or caregivers and children (see section 8.7), there may be times when you can see that they are not acting in the best interest of the child. They may be applying an academic stressor ("My child is not working as hard as they should." "Can you give them more work to better their grade?" "They need to work harder."), or it may be more ominous, like neglect and abuse. In this case, you must involve school personnel, especially the administration. It can provide another source of assistance to address the situation.

8.9. KEEP THE CONVERSATION GOING BUT IN A PERSON-TO-PERSON FORMAT

For some students, it is important to continue the conversation with the parents or caregivers. The continuous contact does not allow for surprises for all those involved. However, these conversations should be in person. As we all know, trying to write what you mean, especially in an email, is much more difficult than saying or explaining what you mean. While the written word helps so we do not have to communicate all our ideas in person, when you must have back-and-forth conversations with parents or caregivers, email becomes cumbersome and opens our ideas to misinterpretation.

Online virtual meetings are also not very effective. Sitting in a chair and talking to a box on the screen does not involve the body language of human communication. Also, how many of us have had discussions or taken classes where, while we are focused on the screen, there are things around our sitting area or on our computer that do not allow for our full attention to the discussion? For these reasons, in-person meetings are important. And while phone conversations are better than email or screen appearances, they still lack the necessary quality focus. Also, for your own protection, be sure you know the state and district laws about situations in which you are mandated to report such incidents to school authorities.

About Others in Your School Community

9.1. YOUR SCHOOL IS A COMMUNITY

You may have seen some writing about schools as institutions, but this idea needs to be questioned. Many years ago, a musical satire stated, "But who wants to live in an institution?" And I believe there is a lot of merit to this question.

Because the school contains people, it is a community. Yes, it has rules to maintain order, allow for safe movement, and more, but it should never be considered an institution. As a community, its primary obligation is the growth of every person involved. Usually in school literature, we speak about the growth of the students and our own growth as professionals. But the question remains, Are these the only two groups of people in the school? Obviously not. There are many people who work to allow the school to run (maybe not as a well-oiled machine, but at least keeps it in motion toward improvement).

My first principal said to me, "There are three people with whom you must be on good terms: The first is me, who will evaluate you. The second is my secretary, who will be very helpful to you as you stumble through your first year. And the third is the head custodian, who can be helpful to you in ways you cannot even know right now." And all this turned out to be true. This became more inciteful to me when he saidd that the head custodian was also the town sheriff. Although I never needed his services in this capacity, it was good to know I knew him, and more importantly, he knew me. But what came across very quickly in my early years was that the three principals for whom I worked saw all their school staff as part of the school. And I saw this in the natural way they interacted with all those who made up the school community.

9.2. IT TRULY TAKES ALL KINDS OF PEOPLE

There is this village called a school, where all people can have an influence on your life. So you need to see them as part of the school community and let them know you recognize them as an integral part in making the school run. Custodians, secretaries, cafeteria workers, school aids, and volunteers all are there because other jobs besides teaching have to be done. They are an integral part of the school, unless you want to clean the rooms, feed the children, and answer phones. And don't forget: A little more than one hundred years ago, teachers had to be in school early in order to stoke the stove to heat the room. So keep this in mind as you move through the school each day.

9.3. THE POWER OF HELLO AND THANK YOU

The hallways of a school are the crossroads of the community. While many people in the school will never enter your classroom, the hallway is where you meet everyone. In your movement around the school, a nod, a smile, and a hello are simple ways to connect with people with whom you normally do not communicate. It is not a matter of making friends but being friendly. And for the nonteaching staff, it is the recognition that you see them as a member of the school community in which they make a difference.

> For you, it is an expansion of your school universe. Do not allow your classroom to become your world. Yes, it is the place where you do your best professional work: that is, teaching. But it is not the only place where your outlook on education as a human endeavor should be seen. It should be seen throughout the school. And there is a good chance that the people of the school community will respond.

9.4. SECRETARIES CAN BE LIFESAVERS
(OR JOB SAVERS), BUT . . .

As stated previously, my first principal told me very early on that there were three people I needed to keep happy, and one was his secretary. The school secretaries are usually major players in a school community. First, they know all the adults in the school, and they see them almost every day. They also know many students in the school, even those students you wish could be with them more often. But sometimes they know them differently. Second, they may be the chief interpreter to the principal about things that happen in the school. They offer an adult noneducational perspective where the educational perspective may not be enough to address an issue. Third, they are the go-to people when there is an emergency. Whether it is major (accident, etc.) or copies needed, they can get things done that you cannot.

Secretaries do not want things done because they want them done. They need them done so they can get their job done. With all the forms you have to fill out and all the paperwork (I guess now we should call it "pixelwork") you have to do, don't blame the secretary. In many cases, the secretary will think like you about all the time spent completing paperwork. So get things done for them. (Leave your professional ego aside for a time.)

And be as helpful as possible. Remember, it is more likely a secretary who creates your letter of reappointment each year and then finally your tenure letter. It's nice to know people in high places.

9.5. CUSTODIANS CAN BE EXTREMELY HELPFUL, SO . . .

As I said, my first principal also told me very early on in my tenure at his school that there were three people I needed to keep happy, and one was the custodian. (He also noted that, with this particular custodian, it would be a good idea because he was also the town sheriff.) Just like a house, keeping a school clean can be a frustrating job because, as you clean it today, you know it will be in a similar circumstance tomorrow. There are few times when you clean a space, and you come back, and it is still clean.

As a teacher, keeping your area clear and orderly takes a few minutes, but it is time well spent. And for the custodial staff, it is just respect. Many times, the custodial staff do not know how to relate to the professional staff. You may find them noncommunicative, but it is often just a matter of them being supercareful of staying within bounds. And while this is important, it should be remembered that, in other circumstances, you could be seen as equals.

Again, as with secretaries, the custodial staff is the go-to group in emergencies. Some incidents may be easy, and others may be not so nice, like cleanup. (If you have experience with lower grades, you know exactly what I mean!) Telling the nonteaching staff that they are an integral part of the school goes a long way in making a community. This is a great message.

9.6. CAFETERIA PERSONNEL

In a school community, there is no group so deep in the background as the cafeteria people. These people may be known in their neighborhood, possibly living next door to teachers, students, or school administrators. But when it comes to school, they can be overlooked. They are there and perform a very important service but for the most part are not seen.

Because they are hidden, it is sometimes difficult to find them, but you should. Decide on something they can help you with (a bottle of water not during lunchtime, a small container of milk for your coffee, etc.). Then, seek them out and *greet them*. Maybe ask how their day is going, kiddingly if they are ready for the students, or how they made it through the onslaught if it is toward the end of the day.

Recognizing people for what they do every day is important in keeping the school community together. No, this is not your major responsibility. That lies elsewhere. However, as one part of the school, it is your responsibility to keep in contact with everyone so that they know you and know that you are just not moving through but instead appreciate their work. It may help them feel good about what they do.

9.7. SUBSTITUTES

If you become ill, you call your doctor. If your doctor is unavailable, you might be sent to a substitute medical doctor. If your lawyer is not available when you are dealing with a legal issue, you may have to work with a substitute attorney who has passed the bar exam. However, in schools, the person called in to substitute for an absent teacher may not be certified, so you need to think in two ways.

First, if the person is going to substitute for you, make sure the work you leave is commensurate with the possibility that they will not be certified and, even if they are, may not be certified in your area, whether it is elementary education or a content area in the secondary school. Make sure the plans are clear and the students will be able to complete the work (or at least come close), even if you have to give the substitute a script to read to the class. Also, remind your students about proper treatment of someone taking your place.

Second, if the person is a substitute for a colleague, you may want to stop by and say hello and ask if they need any assistance. This is not your job, but then again, so much of what you do in a school is not your job, so just add this to the list. For the substitute, a friendly face and the offer of assistance, even when not needed, is a plus at the beginning of a day.

9.8. TEACHERS OF OTHER SUBJECTS OR GRADES

As professionals, we all wish to be respected for what we know and our ability to interact with students as they learn. No matter the content area, there is an expertise that is singularly significant. Make sure you establish respect for those who teach other subjects or grades. At the elementary level, the amount of content may be less because the children at those levels do not have the maturity (cognitive, emotional, or social) to focus academically as children in upper grades do. Just to be clear: Kindergarten takes more expertise in dealing with the maturity of the children than any other. Kindergarten teachers each day go where most in the school fear to tread.

In middle and high school, where the separation of teachers is by subject, be careful of considering some subjects to be minor or those subjects that give students a break. When you hear this from others, it is usually because they truly have no idea what occurs in those content areas. A well-structured program in art, music, and physical education is just as important to the growth of children as a mathematics or reading program. Remember that myriad parts of the brain need to be developed, and there are content areas that approach some but not all. There is a need for classes to address the others. I appreciate knowing something about the music I hear or the artwork I see. In my life, these are not minor. They are parts of all our lives.

9.9. COACHES

The word *coach* projects the image of athletics, but in a vibrant school community, there are many others. You might say that the baseball coach has more status in a school community than a chess coach, but the question is, "Does each perform a vital service in directing students?" The answer must be yes, or there is no reason for their existence. "Does one take more skill than the other?" Well, try to interchange them, and see how that goes.

Coaches in general play a great role in making the school seem more real. In their future lives, students may devote many more hours to what they learned outside the academic classroom, and it may be a great relief from their future careers. This is not about equality of coaches and teachers. Just consider that all play a role in the life of a student. If you are an academic subject teacher, do not let your status get in the way of a good relationship with your colleagues who coach, especially those who do it with scant recognition for what they do for students.

A football coach once said, "If a student does not do well in math, we may take the student off the basketball team. So if a student does not do well in basketball, should we take that student out of math class?" Sounds silly until you think about the whole student.

9.10. SAFETY OFFICERS

The tragic events of the past years have led to a discussion of the presence of safety officers in schools. However, we must remember that safety is not represented by one person. The whole school community must be aware of and participate in the safety of all.

No matter your beliefs on safety officers in the schools, you must support the direction of the school community and include them in your sphere. Whether it is the person at the main door who helps direct visitors, those who provide for efficient movement of the people before and after school, or those who provide for the safety of the children on the grounds of the school during lunch, these people provide a service that you must recognize.

Again it is not an over-the-top recitation of how important they are but just communicating to them that you appreciate that they are there and the work that they do. In this case, a "Hello, how are you?" (see section 9.3) along with a smile is all that it may take. But it needs to be genuine, and it needs to be done.

References

Chapin, Harry. 1988. "My Grandfather." Track 30 on *The Gold Medal Collection.* Elektra Records.

Fulghum, Robert. 1991. *Uh-Oh: Some Observations from Both Sides of the Refrigerator Door.* New York: Vintage Books.

Peters, Tom, and Nancy Green. 2022. *Tom Peters' Compact Guide to Excellence.* Oakton, VA: Ideapress.

Shaw, George Bernard. 1902. *Maxims for Revolutionists.* N.p.: CreateSpace.

INSPIRATIONS

Peters, Tom, and Nancy Austin. 1985. *A Passion for Excellence: The Leadership Difference.* New York: Random House.

Rogers, Fred. 2003. *The World According to Mister Rogers: Important Things to Remember.* New York: Hachette Books.

Ward, G. Kingsley. 1990. *Letters of a Businessman to His Son.* Rocklin, CA: Prima.

About the Author

Frank Gardella has been a classroom teacher and a district K–12 mathematics supervisor. He currently holds the position of associate professor at Hunter College. His career has consistently involved issues faced by new teachers (which he was once himself) and frustrations of veteran teachers. He continues to work with these professionals, offering them a view of teaching that he has developed throughout his career.